Praise for

Winning on Purpose

It is my deepest desire to see every church fruitful, influential, and advancing in God's calling and assignment. The world is crying out for authentic, capable, godly leaders. Winning on Purpose is a tool that can help churches and their pastors to reach their full potential. I highly recommend it.
Dr. Wayne Cordeiro, author of Doing Church as a Team

On rare occasions, there are a few books that must be published, need to be purchased, and definitely should be read. Winning on Purpose is such a book. It provides a new theoretical and practical framework based upon extensive experience for fixing broken congregations and denominations.
Dr. Paul Borden, author of Hit the Bullseye

Kaiser has been there, done that, and has the track record to prove that he knows what he is talking about. Winning on Purpose goes way beyond anything else on the market today in offering concrete, tested, pragmatic steps and insights on how to lead a church through purposeful change. I will be ordering these books by the case, and making them available at all of the events I do. It is that good!
Dr. Dan Southerland, Director, Church Transitions

We live in a world of fast change. If we fear or resist change, we get paralyzed. If we change for change-sake, we can get caught in trends and only confuse people. However, if we think about change in a prayerful, purposeful, and strategic way, we will lead more effectively. Winning on Purpose teaches you exactly how to do that.
Rev. Dan Kimball, author of The Emerging Church

A new wind of the Spirit is blowing through the church. Jesus might have called it "new wineskins." Others call it a second reformation—dealing with how we do church and engage in mission. John Kaiser is a key player in this new thing God is doing and Winning on Purpose is for those committed to becoming a truly missional 21st century church.
Dr. Brian Winslade, National Leader (CEO), Baptist Churches of New Zealand

Winning on Purpose *needs to be an intentional study by every church leader. John Kaiser has taken our weirdness and confusion about responsibility-authority-accountability and replaced it with biblical principles and pragmatic applications. These conversations will bring the church back into alignment with God's mission in the world.*
Rev. Bruce Bugbee, founder, Network Ministries International

John Kaiser is an exceptional thinker and leader. Winning on Purpose provides valuable insights into how churches can achieve their God-given potential.
Dr. Paul Johnson, Senior Vice President, Baptist General Conference

John Kaiser and I have similar passions; we want to see local churches all over North America be all they can be for the Savior. If you're a pastor, Winning on Purpose *is a must read!*
Dr. Aubrey Malphurs, Professor of Pastoral Ministries, Dallas Theological Seminary

Everyone likes to play on a winning team, and every Christian would like to be a part of a winning church. But how can an average church become a winning church? John Kaiser shows us how in this helpful and wise book that every pastor and church board member should read and apply.

Dr. Rick Stedman, Sr. Pastor, Adventure Christian Church, Roseville, California

Kaiser has captured the heart of God and articulated that wisdom in a down-to-earth strategy for churches and ministry organizations. Winning on Purpose provides practical yet biblical ways to change the wineskins of the local church while preserving the wine of the gospel. I highly recommend this book to any church leader.

Rev. Bobby Hill, International Director, Vanguard Ministries

Institutions around the world teach theology and related subjects, and as their graduates hit the trenches it dawns on them they have received little or no training on how to organise and lead the troops! A few may do it intuitively, but most need to be coached. To save yourself a loser's lifetime of frustration, read Kaiser's Winning on Purpose.

Dr. Stuart Robinson, Sr. Pastor, Crossway Baptist Church, Melbourne, Australia

Winning on Purpose is a winner on two accounts: it is practical and usable (or "playable"). What is refreshing is John's credentials—he has played the game himself, and knows how to be a winner. John has planted and grown healthy churches and can write with authority on how to organise congregations to succeed in their mission.

Maj. Kelvin Merrett, Programme Secretary, Australia Southern Territory, Salvation Army

Churches don't normally associate "winning" with ministry. It doesn't sound "spiritual." But we are involved in a cosmic battle for lost lives who matter to God. Kaiser's book can help churches face the battle and win it for the Kingdom.

Dr. Chuck Moore, President, Northern Baptist Seminary

My intention was to do a quick scan of Winning on Purpose. I dove in and didn't come up for air until chapter 4. This is a remarkable book, well-written, and one that deserves a close look by any leader interested in Great Commission ministry. This is the book I will use to prime the pump before our next leadership retreat.

Rev. Ron Browning, Rector, Holy Trinity Anglican Church, Pensacola, Florida

So often the light of our churches is extinguished because we structure them for control and maintenance. I heartily endorse the principles in Dr. Kaiser's book because we have been implementing them over the past three years. Winning on Purpose will help you find the freedom of accountable leadership and the blessing of missional church life.

Dr. Rob Elkington, Sr. Pastor, Faith Baptist Church, Toronto, Canada

As John Kaiser points out in this book, God has already lodged his vote for a prevailing church. Winning on Purpose is a step by step description of the wisdom and work we must embrace to see harvest in our paddock. It is my intention that every person of influence in our church will read this book in the coming year.

Dr. Allan Meyer, Senior Minister, Careforce Church, Melbourne, Australia

Most churches want to be Great Commission and Great Commandment churches, but they don't know how because of the clutter within the church. Winning on Purpose helps remove that clutter by providing a simple frame-of-reference to help almost every new or established church.
Rev. Dave Olson, Director of Church Planting, Evangelical Covenant Church

A guy like John Kaiser bugs me because, like me, he believes in chaordic mission, but he's struck upon a series of extremely helpful tools for harnessing the fierce, untamed force of Christian mission. He offers us rowdy missional types the challenge to be accountable, to be effective, and to grow reproductive, Christ-honouring communities of Faith.
Rev. Michael Frost, Director, Centre for Global Mission, Morling College, Sydney, Australia

I found Winning on Purpose to be easy to read and, although directed toward churches, equally applicable to many organizations with which I have come in contact in my practice of law. I even found myself mentally applying Kaiser's lessons to my own law firm. His book contains valuable lessons for nearly every organization and business.
Mr. J. Brittain Habegger, Attorney-at-Law, Oakland, California

We have been transitioning to a governance board, with little to use as a guide and poor examples of governance within the Anglican Church. As I read Winning on Purpose, my heart and my head were united in a constant chorus of 'yes, that's it.' I am on my second read, eager to warm up for an exciting and fruitful game ahead.
Rev. Drew Mellor, Sr. Pastor, Deep Creek Anglican Church, Melbourne, Australia

Kaiser's extensive experience has allowed him to analyze the structural problems that support dysfunction in churches. This "tell it like it is" book explains the roles of the church board, pastor, and staff, helping the reader to understand the connections between their authority, responsibility, and accountability.
Ms. Debra L. Brown, CEO, Brown Governance Inc.; Chairperson, American Tract Society

"Any enterprise is built by wise planning, becomes strong through common sense, and profits wonderfully by keeping abreast of the facts" Proverbs 24:3-4 (TLB). In Winning on Purpose, Kaiser has given us a "common sense" approach to church organization that meets Solomon's criteria for a profitable enterprise.
Dr. Howard Clark, Sr. Pastor, First Evangelical Church of Memphis, Tennessee

Don't read Winning on Purpose if you believe your call to ministry is an entitlement and the congregation's job is to carry you to retirement. John is a compelling writer who draws deeply from his own well of pastoral and denominational leadership. Read Winning on Purpose if you believe the church at every level must be structured for mission.
Rev. Kenneth R. Bradsell, Director of Operations, Reformed Church in America

John Kaiser first developed his suggestions in the heat of directing a church to reach its mission field and stay focused on missional principles. Now, as a supervisor of congregations, he's fine-tuned those principles for all to utilize. The counsel in this book will guide those who seek to govern their church without losing focus.
Rev. Jim Griffith, Griffith Coaching Network, Denver, Colorado

Winning on Purpose *has provided great information and strategies that help you to aim, structure, and execute an effective strategy for church life and health. If you want to live out a God-sized mission "on-purpose," then read this book!*

Dr. John Jackson, author of PastorPreneur

Winning on Purpose *is an excellent example of the clear thinking Kaiser brings to congregational organisation and leadership. This model has already helped create significant church health in a number of our churches in New Zealand.*

Rev. Lindsay Jones, National Consultant, Baptist Churches of New Zealand

John's book speaks to both principles and practice. His years of experience are scanned into a volume that provides pastors, boards, staff, and members with workable ways forward in a fast-paced and often-confusing world. Winning on Purpose *is biblical, readable, and pragmatic—a book to help leadership teams effectively engage in mission.*

Rev. Stephen Hinks, Director, Leadership Network—Australia and New Zealand

Winning on Purpose *is an indispsnable resource for leaders striving for excellence. Dr. Kaiser has brought together biblical truths with practical steps to an effective missionary strategy for the entire congregation. Every church leader should have a copy of this book in their library.*

Dr. David L. Monk, Sociologist, California State University

In Winning on Purpose *John Kaiser has captured the method needed for pastors and congregations to develop the leadership model needed for health and growth. The marriage of authority, responsibility and accountability allows leaders to transform congregations into missional bodies. This is a must read book for pastors and judicatory leaders.*

Rev. Marvin L. Groote, Executive Congregational Consultant, Presbytery of Utah, PCUSA

There is no shortage of books today on how to turn around a plateaued or declining church. However, if you want to read "the book" that will make a difference in the ministry of your church, then Winning on Purpose *will give you a blueprint that if followed will move your church from dead and dying to a vital mission for Christ.*

Rev. Ken Giacoletto, President, Green Lake Conference Center

We've all experienced dysfunctional structures sucking the life out of the Church's mission. John Kaiser knows what to do about that. His lucid description of "accountable leadership" will spark a turnaround for many congregations.

Rev. Hal Murry, Executive Presbyter, John Knox Presbytery, PCUSA

Winning on Purpose *by John Kaiser is a wonderful blend of scholarship, creativity, and practicality.*

Dr. Ron Rickner, Clinical Psychologist, Tallahassee, Florida

As a competitive person who grew up in and continues to provide ministry coaching within "episcopal" tribal structures, I am especially grateful for Kaiser's Winning on Purpose. *This is an excellent resource for a new congregation.*

Rev. Donald A. Smith, Ministry Coach and Church Planting Strategist, Vital Connections

Winning on Purpose
How to Organize Congregations to Succeed in their Mission

John Edmund Kaiser

Abingdon Press

Nashville

WINNING ON PURPOSE: HOW TO ORGANIZE
CONGREGATIONS TO SUCCEED IN THEIR MISSION

Copyright © 2006 Abingdon Press

This book is printed on recycled, acid-free paper.

Library of Congress Cataloging-in-Publication Data
Kaiser, John Edmund.
    Winning on purpose : how to organize congregations to succeed in their mission / John Edmund Kaiser.
        p.   cm.
    Includes bibliographical references and index.
    ISBN-10: 0-687-49502-4   ISBN-13: 978-0-687-49502-3 (alk. paper)
1. Christian leadership.   2. Missions.   I. Title.

BV652.1.K35   2006
253—dc22

                                                                    2005035551

07 08 09 10 11 12 13 14 15—12 11 10 09 08 07 06 05

MANUFACTURED IN THE UNITED STATES OF AMERICA

To my father

Edmund H. Kaiser, Jr.

for his strength and support

And to the memory of my mother

Callie P. Kaiser

for her love and self-sacrifice

Acknowledgments

FOR THEIR PATIENCE AND ENCOURAGEMENT, I want to thank my beautiful and loving wife, Leonore, and our awesome adult children, Ben and Ruth. For years they have encouraged me to write books. Now that I have begun, they are my biggest cheerleaders. I am very proud of each one of them for their own accomplishments, and I am deeply grateful for the love that we enjoy as a family. Together we have been blessed by God during seasons of success, and together we have been deepened by him during seasons of sorrow. Nothing on earth is more precious to me than my family.

This book is about congregations that set up their pastors for success. It is not possible to mention everyone who has strengthened my hands in ministry. However, I wish to honor three unique friends who stood by me at critical junctures from my first day to my final day as the founding pastor of two congregations: Ben Dady, former vice-president of Florida Power and Light Corp.; Gaylon Fruit, senior pharmacist and business entrepreneur; and Bob Powell, partner in a respected CPA firm. These men have seen me at my best and worst; the last thing any of them could be called is a fair-weather friend.

My single greatest mentor in ministry has been Dr. Paul Borden. His commitment to the integrity of Scripture combined with his strategic thinking to fulfill the Great Commission has resonated deeply with me.

The strategy in this book has been influenced most by Paul Borden's "staff-led model," John Carver's "policy governance model," and Stephen Block's "executive director-concerted model."

Finally, I acknowledge my heroes in the ministry: those rare men and women who invest themselves in service and leadership so that more people can enter into a personal relationship with Christ. May their hearts be strengthened, may their numbers increase, and may their supporters prosper.

John Edmund Kaiser
Sacramento, California

Contents

PART ONE—Do We Really Want to Win?

a reason to exist — the kind of leadership we need — attracting and keeping leaders — a strategy for getting it done

problems of inward focus — problems of anarchy — problems of democracy — problems of oligarchy — problems of hierarchy

the object of the game — the rules of the game — how to keep score — the accountable leadership strategy

PART TWO—Do We Understand the Game?

the source of our objective — Jesus's final word on the matter— Jesus's earlier mission statements — the acts of the (commissioned) apostles — winning at the object of the game

a word of warning about rules — how boundaries work — fair game — breaking the rules — changing the rules

safe and effective organization — when goals are reached — statistics vs. wins — interpretation and application — win, lose, or draw

PART THREE—Do We Know What Position to Play?

diversity on the team — captain of the team — training and coaching for the team

Tables & Figures

FIGURES

Series Foreword

A NEW THEME IS EMERGING in the quest to grow God's mission. Past decades have focused on the importance of *leadership*. In a world that is changing every minute, when programs are being reinvented every week, resources are being redeployed every month, and staff are being retrained every year, *leadership* has been the key to growth for many of the most dynamic mega- and micro-churches today.

Unfortunately, leaders retire, charisma fades, energy flags, ministers are reappointed, and missionaries are called to new mission fields. Leaders are critically important, but they also come and go. The church must continue. The pilgrim band must persist. The body of Christ will always be in motion. Mission can't stop because a leader has disappeared. If it all depends on a leader, the spiritual community of mission movers will soon become an institutional club of innkeepers. If Paul and Peter hadn't prepared for the continuation of the mission to the Gentiles long after their deaths, the Christian movement would never have made it to Cleveland or to the 21st century.

Organization is the emerging theme in the quest to grow God's mission. This is why John's book is so helpful. He helps leaders develop organizations that can outlast them and can also accelerate God's mission into the unknown future. There is a synergy about "leadership" and "organization." The one leads to the other. Great leaders create effective organizations; effective organizations grow great leaders.

The key adjective is the word "effective." The organizations of the established church today are anything but "effective." Originally designed to produce mission results, they have gradually become so complicated and cumbersome as to only produce reports, maintain salaries, and preserve properties. Never has the church managed so much and changed the world so little. Organizations start out as a means to an end; but unless they adapt to the context of mission, they soon become an end in themselves. There is nothing "sacred" about an organization. It is simply a tool.

This book is among the first of an emerging generation of books about church organization. There will be many variations, each customized to deliver mission results in the distinct contexts and changing circumstances of rapidly diversifying cultures. John focuses the fundamental questions that any organizational planner must answer:

- *Do you really want the mission to succeed?* Are you prepared to stake everything, change anything, and do whatever it takes—even if it means altering long and familiar habits, redeveloping precious programs, and redeploying sacred assets?

- *Are you prepared to live within clear boundaries?* Are you prepared to learn the rules, teach the rules, and hold yourself and everyone else accountable to the rules? Can you tell the difference between the essential and the tactical?

- *Are you ready to align yourself with a greater purpose?* Do you understand your role, can you work in a team, and can you invest all your time to deliver the organizational mission—and nothing else? More importantly, are you capable of changing your role and learning new things for the sake of the mission?

- *Do you have what it takes?* Are the resources sufficient, useful, and ready at hand? Have you equipped yourself and your colleagues to confront the known, anticipate the unknown, and learn from inevitable mistakes?

This book helps congregational leaders create an effective organization. It helps you understand the details, shape the strategies, and focus the purpose that will empower your church to get mission results.

Tom Bandy
General Editor, *Convergence* Series

Foreword

THE FAVORITE BIBLE VERSE OF PUBLISHERS, book selling chains, and Internet book distributors has to be Ecclesiastes 12:12, "Of making many books there is no end" (NRSV). Every year, thousands and thousands of books are published and purchased. Some are even read. Many of these titles contribute important pieces to the intellectual, social, and cultural development of the human race. A good number, however, really did not need to be written, are a waste of money if purchased, and contribute only to the death of trees. BUT, on rare occasions there are a few books that must be published, need to purchased, and definitely should be read. *Winning on Purpose* is such a book. It provides a new theoretical and practical framework based upon extensive experience for fixing broken congregations and denominations.

Make no mistake—most North American congregations and denominations are broken, and many of the King's horses and the King's people are finding it impossible to put them back together again. Apart from a few missional congregations that are truly changing their communities and making new disciples for Jesus Christ, most of the thousands of congregations that exist are declining and dying. And of the congregations that are growing, many are doing so at the expense of the wounded and dysfunctional congregations that surround them. The denominations in which most congregations find their home are as broken as the congregations themselves.

Winning on Purpose is clear that any fixing of broken congregations and denominations must start with mission and vision. Failure to start at the beginning will never repair "what needs fixin'." However, many leaders in the ecclesiastical world have led those following to adopt a new mission and embrace a new vision only to see both die like beautiful roses denied water. The reason new life died is that the structure of the congregation or denomination was broken, remains broken, and cannot be made to work. It is time to realize that in a new century, new missions and new visions need to be founded upon new structural concepts that are based upon the life-giving Word of God, not the historical ecclesiastical traditions of godly women and men of old.

When John Kaiser came to the American Baptist Churches of the West, he was struggling with personal ministry experiences where historical structures were sucking the life out of exciting and effective visions. We were experiencing our miracle of transformation. God was blessing congregations with outward focused missions and community changing visions, based upon new structures that honored leadership and demanded accountability. We were focusing on the biblical concepts of leadership, team-led ministries, leaders equipping and laity ministering, and everyone being held accountable as stewards for the production of spiritual fruit. John's thoughtful insight into the issues, connected with the experiences of working with transforming congregations, enabled him both to produce the concepts in this book and to test them in the crucible of real congregations moving from death to life. John was able to take a variety of ideas, concepts, and brainstorms and integrate them into a meaningful system that united mission, vision, values, and structure to produce healthy, growing, and effective congregations. He took what God was doing in ABCW to a whole new level of effectiveness.

We believed that all congregations needed to act like the larger congregations God wanted them to become as they became effective in making more and more disciples. Acting a different size meant becoming staff-led, even for congregations of fifty or less. A staff-led congregation, whether two hundred or two thousand, needs a lay board that allows leaders to lead while they govern. John was able to help us produce such results in congregations of all sizes. The good news is that what he has done so often continues to work with great effectiveness, enabling congregations to achieve their mission and implement their vision. Structure does not dominate, but rather it enhances and allows ministry to grow and flourish. The structure in our congregations allows leaders to lead, staff to manage, boards to govern, and congregations to be involved in significant outward-focused ministries.

I have watched John time after time successfully lead congregations through the changes described in this book. He has led our region, along with other denominational judicatories, to adopt a structure that enhances mission and vision. His message is crucial and fundamental to transformed and reproducing congregations. It is awesome to see him now put into print what he has successfully done orally with congregations, denominations, parachurch, and nonprofit organizations. If you want to know how to implement effective structure in your organization, climb the mountain of reading this book. When you are done and have reached the top, you will have met the guru.

Dr. Paul D. Borden, Executive Minister
American Baptist Churches of the West

Introduction

Though I am free and belong to no one,
I have made myself a slave to everyone, to win as many as possible . . .
I have become all things to all people so that by
all possible means I might save some.
I do all this for the sake of the gospel, that I may share in its blessings.
Do you not know that in a race all the runners run,
but only one gets the prize?

Run in such a way as to get the prize.

Everyone who competes in the games goes into strict training.
They do it to get a crown that will not last;
but we do it to get a crown that will last forever.
Therefore I do not run like someone running aimlessly;
I do not fight like a boxer beating the air.
No, I strike a blow to my body and
make it my slave so that after I have preached to others,
I myself will not be disqualified for the prize.

The Apostle Paul, 1 Corinthians 9:19–27 (TNIV)

IN *THE UNTOUCHABLES*, A MOVIE ABOUT ELLIOTT NESS AND AL CAPONE, a crusty old cop named Jimmy Malone asks Ness the same question three times. When Malone (played by Sean Connery, whose rich baritone voice and muffled consonants drip with character) is recruited, he looks Ness in the eye and asks, "What are you prepared to do?" testing to see if Ness can be trusted to go the distance against Capone. When the case against Capone hits a dead end and Malone wants to know if Ness is willing to go beyond conventional police work to get him, he asks Ness, "And what are you prepared to do, now?" And when Malone lies dying from machine gun wounds on the floor of his flat, he pulls Ness close, and gurgles, "What . . . are you . . . prepared . . . to do?"

When I read 1 Corinthians 9:19–27, I think of Jimmy Malone. The Apostle Paul was the kind of leader that Malone would have trusted and followed, come hell or high water. Paul had the combination that the Irish veteran was looking for: dedication to the mission, the character not to compromise his integrity on the job, and the audacity to use any means necessary—within his integrity—to win against the enemy.

This book is for readers who want their congregations to succeed in mission and therefore want their pastors to succeed in leadership. That can include board members looking for a way to lend support without rubber-stamping, pastors looking for a way to lead boldly without lording it over people, denominational executives looking for way to recruit effective pastors, consultants looking for a way to help ministries move to the next level, and dedicated church members looking for a way to understand how their congregation can thrive. For all of these readers and more, the chapters that follow offer such a way: a strategy for mission that can make a measurable difference in results. It's not for everybody…only for those who play to win on purpose.

After ten years as an active volunteer and twenty-three years in full-time ministry, I know from experience that not all ministers play to win. Some run aimlessly. Some beat the air with their fists. These men and women either don't know or don't care that, having preached to others, they themselves may be disqualified for the prize. Every time I see a pastor who avoids taking risks in order to keep a job, a board member who undercuts the pastor's authority in order to keep control, or a church member who whines about new Christians in order to keep them from "taking over our church,"—I want to shout, *It doesn't have to be this way!*

Rather than curse against the dark, however, I choose to light a candle. *Winning on Purpose* is a way to organize congregations for success in mission. All this talk of success in the church is bound to stir up a few questions for thoughtful readers. Since there is no space to answer them all, I want to acknowledge up front four assumptions that underlie this book:

God wins on purpose and wants his Church to do the same.

As early as the curse in Genesis 3:15, God has been out to crush the head of the Serpent. In Mel Gibson's film, *The Passion of the Christ,* you can even hear it *crunch.* Winning is not always nice, but winning by the right side is always good. In Matthew 16:18, Jesus describes his Church on the offense, battering down the gates of hell.

Fruitfulness is the same theme of prevailing dressed in a different biblical metaphor. Images such as the sower in Matthew 13 and the vine branches in John 15 depict the deepest, most intimate, and most God-glorifying disciples as those who "bear much fruit." Thinking of success in the church is neither an encroachment of corporate business culture nor an inherently modern fixation of Boomers. Even the sports metaphor in *Winning on Purpose* dates back as far as 1950—1950 years ago that is. See Paul fight. See Paul run. Run, Paul, run. The emphasis of this image in 1 Corinthians 9:19–27 is not on the discipline of training but on the purpose for the discipline, which is to win the race.

Wait—doesn't God love losers? Of course! In moral terms, all of us sons of Adam and daughters of Eve are losers. But God doesn't love us because we're losers. And his love doesn't leave us as losers. God is the Ultimate Winner, and he makes a place for us on the winning side. The name of his team is not Losers Anonymous, it is Those Who Overcome. God has a redemptive purpose in the world and is serious about prevailing. This positive view of triumph, though not triumphalism, is a key assumption of this book.

We win by using God's gifts for God's purposes.

Congregations don't win by sporting the largest auditorium any more than sports teams win by congregating in the largest stadium. Congregations and teams win by reaching the goal. It may well be that winning teams tend to have better stadiums and that winning congregations tend to have better auditoriums, but don't confuse the consequence with the cause.

Success is achieving an intended outcome. Success in God's Church is achieving the outcome God intends. Another word for this outcome is *mission*. Just as essential as reaching the goal is reaching the goal without cheating. In other words, as we press toward the mark using all possible means, true winners in ministry are committed to operating within the bounds of God's revealed Word, the Bible. That commitment does not limit us to the strategies and tactics of the prophets and the apostles, but it does limit us to their value system.

Speaking of strategies and tactics, we recognize with James 1:17 that all good gifts come down from the Father, who provides us with natural and spiritual gifts and then empowers us when we use our gifts for his purposes. Christ will build his Church. However, one thing that God does not provide is foolishness. That's a human contribution. When we reach a critical mass of foolishness by neglecting God's mission and squandering God's gifts, we should not be surprised when Christ builds his Church through some other congregation instead of through ours.

Groups cannot normally be expected to lead or be held accountable.

Paul Borden, Executive Minister of the American Baptist Churches of the West, offers a theory on this point in his book, *Hit the Bullseye:* "It is impossible to hold groups of people accountable, unless you are willing to dismiss the entire group when expectations are not met. I believe one of the main reasons that ecclesiastical bodies like committees and commissions is that these groups are ways for people to have influence without being held accountable, because we are usually unwilling to tell a group that it can no longer exist."[1]

Bodies of believers such as congregations, small groups, ministry teams, and the like are the building blocks for expanding the community of Christ on earth. Many failures in ministry result from individualism, rugged or otherwise, crowding out the corporate nature of the Christian mission. Together we are infinitely more than the sum of our parts because together we are the body of Christ. However, despite our status as a body—no, scratch that—*because* of our status as a body, we must value the unique contribution of each individual part, including leaders. A hand is not the eye. A sheep is not the shepherd. And a board member is not the pastor. Leading is merely a specialty of service, not a badge of honor. Every obedient servant of God is worthy of honor, but not every servant is called and gifted for effective pastoral leadership.

The reliance on accountable, individual leadership may well be the most controversial assumption underlying *Winning on Purpose*. It runs counter to the preference for team and community favored by some respected writers addressing current postmodern/emergent/missional issues. For this reason it also runs the risk of *ad hominem* criticism as a limited "Modern" or "Boomer" perspective. Easum and Travis's *Beyond the Box,* for example, devotes its first chapter to the opposite position: "Beyond One-Person Leadership: Shifting to Teams." The authors are influential thinkers and, ironically, effective leaders and developers of leaders. However, I must respectfully disagree with their initial argument because I believe it dismantles a straw man. The book is filled with examples of effective and innovative congregations. However, none of them, including those cited in the first chapter, lacks an effective lead pastor. I could not ask for a better compilation of evidence for my conviction on the need for a leader. Those who differ on this point are in good company and may nevertheless gain some helpful insights from parts of my book while rejecting its central premise. However, for an organizational model based on teams in place of leaders, one must look elsewhere, such as Tom Bandy's *Christian Chaos*. The present volume seeks without apology to set up congregations for success in mission by setting up their pastors for success in leadership.

This book is adaptable to a wide range of contexts.

The Church of Jesus Christ finds expressions in a vast array of denominations around the world. Each one has a history and a polity, either formal or assumed. Most denominations recognize at least a few of the others. Some claim to be the one true denomination. Other identifiable groups of congregations deny that they are denominations. Finally, there are churches that find denominations divisive, so they are *nondenominational,* ironically dividing themselves from everyone.

This book is written with a wide variety of Christian movements in mind. The strategy of "Accountable Leadership," as I have called it in my training and consulting, is applicable and adaptable to virtually any organization that is serious about accomplishing a mission. This scope goes beyond any one Christian polity, whether traditional or emerging. As theory, it can be adapted beyond Christianity or beyond religious entities of any kind. However, by design this volume is written specifically as a tool for Christian congregations who are committed to fulfilling the mandate of Christ to make disciples of all nations.

It is my intention to offer a strategy that can be customized for traditional, contemporary, or emergent ministries without prejudice. It is not my intention to address the process of change, except in passing, or to advocate for one polity or movement over another. I have made an effort to touch on the problems and uniquenesses of the four broad streams of episcopal, presbyterian, and congregational polity, and emerging "unpolity." The brevity of this book does not allow for the complexities of these broad streams to be addressed, much less the nuances of the individual movements that constitute each stream. My remarks in this regard are meant to be suggestive starting points only.

The organizational strategy I have developed is called "Accountable Leadership." Though the strategy has been influenced by interaction with the systems of many others including John Carver, Stephen Block, Cyril Houle, and Tom Bandy, readers would be mistaken to view *Winning on Purpose* as a presentation of or argument for any of these models.[2]

Accountable Leadership differs in systemic ways from each of them. The strategy has been used across denominations in the United States, New Zealand, and Australia but has been implemented most through the American Baptist Churches of the West, based in California. In this book, it is presented one layer at a time as the answers to four broad questions for congregations and their pastors:

1) Do we really want to win?
   A foundation of intentionality, difficulties, and strategy

2) Do we understand the game?
   Three dynamic elements of the task to understand

3) Do we know what position to play?
   Four components of the model to align

4) Do we have the right equipment?
   A collection of tools for implementation

For congregations that want to prevail, I would say Jimmy Malone asks the big question, and the Apostle Paul supplies the right answer. *What are you prepared to do?* "Run in such a way as to get the prize."

Notes

1. Paul Borden, *Hit the Bullseye: How Denominations Can Aim the Congregation at the Mission Field* (Nashville: Abingdon Press, 2003), 127. "Like" is a verb in this sentence.
2. See each author's work in the Annotated Bibliography.

PART ONE

DO WE REALLY WANT TO WIN?

CHAPTER ONE
Playing to Win Beats Playing Around

Everyone has a purpose in life. Perhaps yours is watching television.
David Letterman

WHEN YOU PICK UP A PING-PONG PADDLE, especially if it has been a while, it's fun just to volley back and forth with your opponent for a few minutes without keeping score. There's no pressure to perform, no pressure to keep the rules, and—most importantly—no pressure to win. Plus, going through the motions to warm up prepares you to play a better game. At some point though, either you or your opponent is bound to say, "Ready? Let's play for real."

According to Lyle Schaller, in the United States there are over 300,000 Protestant congregations, all of them presumably going through the motions of "having church" in one form or another.[1] How many of them are winning the hearts and minds of people in their communities for Jesus Christ? How many of them are even keeping score? How many of them are just enjoying their little volley as an end in itself?

A Reason to Exist

The first question for any band of believers who cares about their collective destiny is this: *Why does our congregation exist?* Before we look at the possible answers, let's make sure we understand the question. The question is not why the Church of Jesus Christ exists. The question is not why we as humans or as Christians exist. The question before us is more local and more urgent: Why does *our congregation* exist? If Community Church of Ourtown, that we attend, were to disappear, what difference would it make? More pointedly, *for whom* would it make a difference?

For congregations in local communities, there are only three possible answers to this question:[2]

1) This congregation exists for us—the people inside.

2) This congregation exists for others—the people outside.

3) This congregation exists for both.

The first answer obviously reflects a congregation with an inward focus. Caring for its own members is the primary task. According to missiologist Win Arn, 89% of church attendees surveyed said that the primary purpose of their congregation is to serve their needs and the needs of their family.[3] So in practice, if not in print, it may be fair to say that most congregations choose Answer #1.

A minority of congregations that put outreach first choose Answer #2. Whether they do it through traditional altar calls, contemporary seeker services, or postmodern community ministries, the primary customers to be served are the people who "aren't here yet." These congregations are fully outward in their focus.

But there is a third option: *We are here for everybody.* Hard to argue with this position, isn't it? It appeals to our general sense of fair play, not to mention the character of God, who "does not show favoritism" (Acts 10:34, TNIV). When we look closely at the Great Commission in Matthew 28:19–20, we see that as Jesus's disciples, we are not only to make and baptize more disciples but also to teach them once we have them. Evangelize *and* edify. Know Christ *and* make Christ known. What could be more biblically, theologically, and politically correct than to say that our congregation exists to serve *both* the people inside and the people outside? What could possibly be wrong with Answer #3?

Nothing.

It's a safe answer. It isn't wrong. But it isn't sufficient either. If we say that our congregation is here to serve both the insider and the outsider, we are compelled to ask a follow-up question: Who will we serve *first*? Now if at this point we try to achieve the overrated virtues of balance and lack of controversy, we will discover a surprise. If we say that we will serve both groups equally, you may be sure that our congregation will wind up hopelessly focused inward. How so? Because the needs of those inside the congregation are the ones that will always be in your face. The squeaky wheel gets the grease, and if there is one spiritual gift that all congregations have, it is the gift of squeaking with tongues. *Why don't we ever sing my favorite songs? Why didn't someone visit me when I was sick? Why don't we have a children's club for my third grader?* However, no one will ever march down the street from the neighborhood, pound on the pastor's office door, and demand, "Why haven't you started making disciples of Jesus Christ on my block?!"

If we fail to put both intention and resources behind the mission of serving others before serving ourselves, we will not escape the gravitational force of inwardness. Self-centered behavior is the human condition, and it cannot be overcome without submission to divine priorities and power.

On the other hand, when a congregation chooses Answer #3 and then goes on to choose serving others first and themselves second, it is embarking on an outward-focused ministry that also takes care of its own. The primary vs. secondary priority is essential to an outward focus despite the fact that the nature of the serving differs according to the need of those served. The need of outsiders to be reached must be raised noticeably higher than the need of the members to be equipped for reaching them. Otherwise, the equipping easily becomes code for inward preoccupation. The mission of Christ to the world comes first, and supporting the mission team comes second but not far behind.

The Kind of Leadership We Need

Once we profess that our congregation exists first to bring others into relationship with Jesus Christ, we have addressed the question of mission. To be a missional congregation is to be an outward-focused congregation. But how are we going to accomplish that mission?

Mission statements and vision statements are good starting points. While sometimes used interchangeably, I find it most helpful to use *mission* to define our purpose and *vision* to describe what that purpose might look like when it is fulfilled in our unique context. Creating these statements helps us sort out and disseminate what is most important to us as a body. Nevertheless, there is nothing more common in stagnant congregations than pithy mission slogans. Bulletin covers, bookmarks, and bumper stickers do not a mission make.

What, then, is the factor separating mission *articulated* from mission *accomplished?* That critical factor is the organizational culture of the congregation, which is woven from its deepest values—not some list of "core values" on display in the foyer but the real and rarely admitted priorities that determine how money, time, and attention are distributed.

If terms like "values" and "organizational culture" seem too abstract at this point, let me put them into a parable:

> The board of a certain congregation decided that reaching teenagers in the neighborhood would be part of its vision for a new commitment to outward-focused mission. So they initiated a recreation program at the church on Friday nights. Volunteers were trained not only to keep the fun and

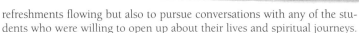

refreshments flowing but also to pursue conversations with any of the students who were willing to open up about their lives and spiritual journeys.

Six weeks into the new program, the board met again to evaluate and learned that three things had happened: 1) a young woman had become a Christian, 2) a young man had agreed to meet regularly with the youth pastor to explore Christianity, and 3) a window in the church had been broken. The board concluded, "That recreation night was such a great idea! Too bad it didn't work. Obviously we can't have windows being broken, so let's phase out the program and send more money to Young Life. They are better equipped to deal with these kids."

Now what kind of logic leads to a board decision like this? Is keeping the church property in excellent condition a good thing? Sure. Is helping local teenagers come to Christ a good thing? Certainly. One more question: *Which is more important?* This is what I mean by the kind of values that form an organizational culture. A value is not a choice between a good thing and a bad thing. It is a choice between two good things, based on the priority we give to them—usually a hidden priority. We would never say that facility upkeep is more important than the eternal destiny of a high school student, but congregations *operate* from values like this one, week in and week out.[4]

On the other hand, if the board were to align its values to its mission, a different kind of logic would result: "Hmm. If we can get one and a half conversions for every broken window, let's set a goal next year of breaking every window in the church! We can always buy more glass."

The organizational culture is made up of deeply held priorities that either line up with an outward-focused mission and vision or else automatically undermine them. By its very nature, a mission requires a change from the status quo. For most congregations, this change must be systemic change at the level of culture, not just incremental change at the level of activities.

If you believe that mission happens naturally in congregations through business as usual, then the only kind of pastoral leadership you need is *operational leadership:* someone to preach the Word, conduct services, oversee programs, and keep the campers happy. If, however, you believe that mission happens only through the courage to continually realign an organization's culture with the values of Christ, then you need something more in a pastor. You need *transformational leadership.*

Attracting and Keeping Leaders

When a congregation that has been declining or has plateaued is looking for a new pastor to turn things around, a warning is in order: "Any pastor smart enough to turn this congregation around is smart enough not to come here." Good leadership goes where good leadership is supported. And any pastor who is a leader knows that a stagnant congregation, regardless of its size, is not a congregation with a high value on strong pastoral leadership—at least not lately. A high value on strong pastoral leadership is central to the strategy in this book.

Have you ever wondered why we don't have a greater number of excellent candidates to choose from when electing public officials? Take a look at what those women and men have to go through to get and to keep those positions. Every detail, both old and new, of their lives is paraded on the evening news. They have to raise and spend a fortune just to get in the door. Then they contend with bureaucracy, media, and public opinion. Who wants to live like that? We're lucky to find an excellent choice every now and then. No wonder so many of the best leaders go into business, where their achievements stand a better chance of recognition and reward.

Now think about what transformational pastors have to go through to lead a congregation into mission. Seminary, if they go that route, requires three years of graduate study beyond a bachelor's degree plus an internship, a thesis, or both—all at private school tuition rates. Then they are called to serve a congregation where their judgment and motives are constantly second-guessed. Their family lives in a fishbowl on display. And when they begin to exercise missional leadership to make all the sacrifices worthwhile, the board insists in high spiritual tones that pastors run everything by them, if not the whole congregation, for approval. "It's for your own protection," the board tells pastors. What they don't tell pastors is that it's protection from the board itself.

A competent leader in many arenas of life is often treated as an asset, but a competent leader in pastoral ministry is often treated as a child—and a problem child at that. If we want more winners in pastoral ministry overall, and if we especially want a winner as the pastor of our particular congregation, then we had better find a way to set up leaders for success instead of frustration.

The win we fundamentally desire and believe that God desires is not the success of pastors per se but the success of local congregations in fulfilling the mission Christ has given them. However, if it takes a transformational pastor to lead us there, then we need a strategy to attract a leader, to support a leader, and even to replace a pastor who proves not to be a leader. The good news is that if we properly support leaders, the attraction and replacement issues may largely take care of themselves.

Shepherds who lead their flocks—not exactly an innovative concept for the 21st century, is it? No—but we will have to introduce a winning strategy in order to implement this authentic biblical leadership concept in our third-millennium context. That's what this book is all about. Ready? Let's play for real.

SUMMARY & PREVIEW

- *It's time to get serious about the reason our congregation exists.*
- *If we're serious about this mission, we need the right leadership to achieve it.*
- *If we're serious about leadership, we need to attract and support it.*
- *If we're serious about supporting leadership, we need a strategy for doing so.*

The next chapter identifies five sets of obstacles that keep various congregations from winning. These problems stem from both historical and functional forms of church government. Problems that arise from inward focus, anarchy, democracy, oligarchy, and hierarchy will be discusssed. Later in the book we will see how the Accountable Leadership strategy can counter these problems.

Notes

1. Lyle Schaller, *The Very Large Church,* (Nashville: Abingdon, 2000), 42.
2. I am indebted to Paul Borden for the basic outline of this presentation, which he uses often in training seminars.
3. Rick Warren, *The Purpose-Driven Church,* (Grand Rapids: Zondervan, 1995), 82.
4. I created this story a few years ago, thinking it was a little extreme but to the point. Recently a seminar participant surprised me by claiming that it happened for real in his congregation—not over a broken window but over half-eaten hot-dogs left out on the stairs. He wondered what else I knew about his church board!

CHAPTER TWO
The First Step is to
Stop Defeating Ourselves

Only two things are infinite,
the universe and human stupidity,
and I'm not sure about the former.
Albert Einstein

I ONCE HEARD RALPH NEIGHBOR, JR. say, "God forgives all kinds of sin, but stupid is forever." In this chapter, we'll explore five forever-stupid sets of problems that we church leaders face, all of our own making. No congregation shares them all, but most congregations have more than their share.

A word of perspective is in order before we survey our ecclesiastical foibles. Though the groupings of problems are organized below somewhat by broad traditions of polity (with the exception of inward focus, which is universal), all congregations may be susceptible to nearly any problem touched upon in this chapter. There are dynamics of anarchy, democracy, oligarchy, and hierarchy at work in all congregations and denominations. Nevertheless, polity does affect which kinds of problems occur more frequently.

Problems of Inward Focus

It's hard to win if you're not in the game.

This first set of problems stems not from the particular history or polity of a group but from human nature. Inward focus is the one set of problems to which congregations of every tribe are susceptible. In the absence of intentional leadership to the contrary, a congregation will focus most, if not all, of its resources away from evangelism and onto itself. We have developed any number of rationalizations for neglecting the mission of Christ. So how do the problems of inward focus show up in the church?

1) *The Great Commission, to make disciples, is displaced by other good pursuits.* Depending on the group, these pursuits may include creating positive peer groups for kids, teaching the Bible, opposing social evils, overcoming past hurts, creating a powerful worship experience, helping the poor, developing spiritual disciplines, building deep

friendships, supporting missionaries, correcting deficient theology, deconstructing modernity, associating with good groups, disassociating from bad groups, supporting our educational mode of choice, and preserving church heritage. These good pursuits can support the mission if subordinated to it. If not, they compete with the mission and help us to feel good even as we neglect the mission.

2) *Putting the desires of insiders first leads to divisions based on opposing special interest groups.* The most notorious example of this problem would be the style of music used in worship services. Each generation and culture is tuned to a different set of frequencies, rhythms, and decibels. Whose favorite will we approve for use in church? The real question is, "How should we decide?" An outward-focused congregation bases the choice on its mission field. We can sing music we don't like for the purpose of bringing people to Jesus. But what does the ingrown church base its choice on? Majority rule? Golden Rule (whoever gives the gold makes the rules)? Whether it's music or some other point of contention, focusing outward gives us a cause worthy of sacrifice. Focusing inward makes us the cause.

3) *In the absence of biblical mission, the congregation suffers a lack of vision, which leads it to plateau and decline.* Churches have life cycles just like people do. They are born, they grow, they mature, they decline, and they die. The tipping point that flips a congregation from the upward side of the life cycle to the downward side is not poor organizational structure, troubled relationships, or weak programs; it is the loss of vision. Problems with programs, people, and policies are the result of inadequate vision. When individuals can see no compelling destination to which all the church activities are leading, they are understandably less willing to show up and pay up. It's not a lack of commitment; it's the lack of a cause that is worthy of commitment.

Problems of inward focus cause us to defeat ourselves because they keep us out of the game to begin with. If we are preoccupied with the color of our uniforms, the time practice starts, and which band plays at the team party, we may forget that the whole reason we suit up, work out, and celebrate is to play the game and win on purpose.

Problems of Anarchy

It's hard to win if no one is sure who's picking the plays.

Structure in the congregation often gets bad press from those who feel it is antithetical to spirituality. The church is an organism, not an organization, right? The church is described in the New Testament as an army, a building, a field, a temple, a bride, a body, a flock, a family, a people, a vineyard, a priesthood, a letter, and an olive tree, among other things. Each of these images captures part of the essence of the church. Some of them are organic; some are inorganic. We can either say that the church is an organized organism like a body (each part with a function distinct and related to the others), or an organic organization like a family or an army (a matrix of living beings). Either way, the church is not a spiritual invertebrate. Nevertheless, from time to time there are movements seeking to point us back to "New Testament Christianity" in a way that casts suspicion on formal organization. When this impulse is carried too far, it creates a particular set of obstacles for a congregation trying to achieve its mission:

1) *When we aim at nothing in particular, that's what we hit.* Rigidity can be a problem in excess, but so can flexibility. Ministry without structure is like crude oil. Crude oil is shapeless and can be refined into any number of useful products, but in its raw state it is no more than a slippery mess. Congregations that eschew an appropriate level of structure can be just as sloppy and useless.

2) *Movements seeking to restore "New Testament Christianity" often overlook cultural and missional contextualization in both the first and the twenty-first centuries.* Early gatherings of the church often used the format of a synagogue, not because it was "biblical" but because it was indigenous. While scholars reasonably speculate about origins of the synagogue during the Exile, there is no historical reference to the synagogue prior to the time of Jesus, when we find it fully formed and empire-wide. So God did not prescribe the synagogue in the Old Testament or the New. Nevertheless, by the first century it was an accepted form of gathering that allowed the early church to adapt its mission effectively in Jewish quarters of the Greco-Roman world. Much criticism of so-called "secular" practices in the church fails to appreciate North America, Europe, and similar societies as mission fields for which the gospel must be faithfully contextualized.

3) *Without a structure for accountability, the most dysfunctional people often shape the life of a congregation.* Healthy congregations are magnets for healthy people and are medicine for needy people. Needy congregations are magnets for needy people and medicine for no one. If there is no system to reinforce productive behavior and correct destructive

behavior, the center of influence may well gravitate to those most willing to coerce the congregation through money or relationships. Broken structure provides poor accountability; absent structure provides none at all.

4) *Lack of intentional structure will facilitate the path of least resistance, which is inward focus.* Like gravity, inward focus in the church is a constant force. Gravity can be overcome through the effort to design, build, pilot, fuel, and maintain a complex structure called an airplane. Overcoming inwardness in a congregation requires a similar level of intentionality. In its absence, the members will succumb to the comfort zone and make few new disciples of Jesus Christ. Lack of structure facilitates such inward focus.

5) *Even with an outward focus by intention, a ministry without structure is unlikely to make much impact.* If a person has a sincere desire to cross a great river but lacks a suitable structure like a bridge or a ferry, he or she may plunge in only to be swept away by the current. Two church plants that I have observed up close (one in California and one in Western Australia) both eschew strategy and structure as incompatible with their concept of "incarnational" ministry. Both are doing good, but neither is doing well. They are outward-focused, and for that they deserve support and admiration. However, the good they can do is quite limited. They are making few disciples in the short-term, and I fear that they will not make any once their struggling pastors give up one day—not for lack of good intentions but for lack of good support structures.

Anarchy in the church causes us to defeat ourselves because it keeps us from playing strategic positions on the team. In reaction to *dysfunctional* structures, we may fail to create the *missional* structures that we need to define goals, identify boundaries, and keep score of wins.

Problems of Democracy

It's hard to win if everybody picks the plays.

Congregationalism is a tradition that arose indirectly from the Reformation. Neither Luther, Calvin, nor Zwingli taught congregational rule for the church, but each of them promoted the priesthood of all believers. This doctrine broke with centuries of precedent in the Church of Rome, which claimed to connect people with Christ exclusively through the hierarchy of ordained clergy in apostolic succession. The Anabaptists in continental Europe and later the Separatists in Elizabethan England took the break a step further to deny any spiritual authority over the local congregation other than Christ himself. In 1639, Roger Williams founded the first Baptist church in America (though hardly the last "first" Baptist church in America) halfway through his spiritual pilgrimage from Anglican priest to independent "Seeker."[1] With the creation of the U.S. Constitution one hundred and fifty years later, the democratic spirit of Williams' "soul liberty" became nearly synonymous with the American way of life. As important as every member is to the body of Christ, congregational polity comes with its share of obstacles to accomplishing mission:

1) *Congregational rule is notorious for divisive politics.* The church "split" is not unique to movements with congregational polity, but it has been elevated to an art form by them. Even when a split does not result, deciding the direction of a ministry in the atmosphere of a town hall meeting can be debilitating to the unity of a congregation. *Roberts' Rules of Order* is designed to referee with an even hand the most vicious debates between people with opposing values. When it is imposed on the body of Christ, however, it has the awkward effect of lining up all the red cells on one side and all the white cells on the other. The body attacks itself, as in arthritis or organ rejection, and there is often no need for the Enemy of the Church to lift a finger.

2) *The agenda of a democratic congregation has difficulty rising above the lowest common denominator of spiritual maturity.* The default orientation for all of us in a congregation is to meet our own needs. Often as an afterthought, we meet the needs of others who need Christ. Sanctification is the lifelong process of reversing these priorities so we become selfless like Jesus. However, a congregation normally represents a wide spectrum of spiritual maturity. If the majority sets the standard for our ministry, it should not be surprising to find that standard set fairly low, based on pleasing ourselves, rather than set higher, based on lifting our eyes to see the harvest.

3) *A democratic church culture is fertile ground for controllers.* The pastor of one declining Baptist congregation in the Midwestern U.S. brought me in as a consultant to conduct an assessment. After agreeing with the strengths, weaknesses, and areas for change, the diaconate voted unanimously to recommend my prescription to the congregation. Within a couple of weeks, however, a couple recently removed from leadership and not present for the assessment began to recruit opposition. Some

diaconate members who were long-term friends of this couple pushed for a secret ballot at the upcoming congregational meeting so that they could vote against their own recommendation without anyone knowing. In the end, the pastor chose to withdraw the proposal so that he could live to lead another day. There were no means available in the system to keep controllers from holding the church hostage.

4) *A vision for the future that arises from a committee of the whole is fragmented, fuzzy, and unstable.* Insects have compound eyes and process the multiple images into data they can use, but people don't function like that. We work best when we have a single image with depth perception. When direction is designed by a group, its clarity will be compromised and changeable from vote to vote.

5) *Congregational churches tend to leave ministry to the pastor and leadership to the members.* Equipped congregations, in terms of Ephesians 4:11–16, do just the opposite. On the positive side, groups with a heritage of grassroots involvement enjoy a value on the priesthood of believers that can be redeemed for every-member-ministry.

Problems of Oligarchy

It's hard to win if a committee picks the plays.

In 1561 John Knox produced the *Book of Discipline* for Scotland, which systematized the presbyterian polity John Calvin used in Geneva, where Knox once found refuge from persecution.[2] Out of this heritage come two forms of presbyterian polity used today: *connectional* and *independent* presbyterian polity. Knox and Calvin both endorsed the connectional variety: each congregation led by a pastor and group of elders, who are accountable to a higher *presbytery*, which is accountable to a *synod* and in turn to a *general council*. This hierarchy of courts stands in contrast to the independent version of presbyterian polity, in which the congregation is ruled by a "plurality of elders" who are not accountable to any human authority. There are benefits in gathering spiritual leaders to set direction and offer wise counsel. However, presbyterian polity brings inherent weaknesses to mission just as other polities do:

1) *The use of selected biblical titles in presbyterian polities tends to camouflage adherence to biblical principles.* In congregations with presbyterian polity, people occasionally make comments to this effect: "We believe in biblical church government; we have an elder board." Aside from the fact

that no congregation in biblical times ever had a board of any kind, calling a board member an elder doesn't make him one—or *her* either, depending on the denomination. In the New Testament, three Greek words are used for the same leaders: *episkopos* (overseer, supervisor, bishop), *presbuteros* (elder), and *poimen* (pastor, shepherd). Would elder-ruled congregations feel as biblical if they had a "board of bishops or a "board of supervisors" instead? Do they expect the same preparation, calling, and time from an "elder" that they do from a "pastor"? The answer to these questions is probably no. Why does it matter? Because if using a favorite biblical *term* obscures how well we are applying an important biblical *principle,* our polity has gotten in the way of our obedience.

2) *Congregations ruled by elders often assume that their polity mirrors the New Testament church and is therefore sacred.* To be fair, this mistake may also be made in congregational and episcopal groups. However, in my experience it is more commonplace with elder boards—especially within conservative evangelical movements. The more rigid and doctrinaire a congregation is about its claim to biblical structure, the less likely it is to adjust and adapt that structure to the challenges of mission in a rapidly changing world.

3) *For congregations with independent presbyterian polity, the elders tend to be accountable to no one but themselves.* In connectional presbyterian polity, the elder board or *session* is moderated by the pastor, and both are technically accountable to a higher court, the *presbytery*. Therefore, this point of critique is not directed primarily to presbyterian *denominations*. However, in movements composed of autonomous local churches that practice presbyterian polity *within* but *not among* the congregations, the board functions as a true oligarchy—a law unto itself. Elders reappoint themselves or select their successors, sometimes with and sometimes without routine congregational confirmation. As President Andrew Johnson once said, "Tyranny and despotism can be exercised by many, more rigorously, more vigorously, and more severely, than by one." Meaningful accountability can be as scarce in churches as it is reputed to be in government and education. Elder-rule in an autonomous church may well be the least accountable polity of all.

4) *Elder boards easily mistake groupthink for the voice of the Holy Spirit.* The 1986 explosion of the Challenger was found to have resulted from good people with the best intentions making a bad decision about O-rings due to *groupthink*. Yale social psychologist Irving Janis defined

groupthink as "a mode of thinking that people engage in when they are deeply involved in a cohesive in-group, when the members' strivings for unanimity override their motivation to realistically appraise alternative courses of action." Janis identified eight symptoms of groupthink that sound as if he spent his career studying elder boards: illusion of invulnerability, belief in inherent morality of the group, collective rationalization, out-group stereotypes, self-censorship, illusion of unanimity, direct pressure on dissenters, and self-appointed mindguards.[3] Boards composed of nonvocational volunteers with limited time and energy easily become isolated, impatient, insulated, and self-justifying. They may compile their collective intuition instead of searching the Scriptures on church-altering decisions—seeking to "hear what God is saying" to them instead of seeking to obey what God's Word has clearly said to everyone.

Problems of Hierarchy

It's hard to win if bureaucrats pick the plays. What do Catholic, Orthodox, Anglican, Methodist, Salvation Army, Church of God (Cleveland), and Foursquare groups have in common? Bishops. Their tradition of apostolic authority over pastors brings upsides and downsides. Here are some of the latter:

1) *In an explicitly hierarchical denomination, mission tends to be displaced by institutional distinctives, whether intellectual reflection, liturgical purity, charismatic experience, or social activism.* Movements with other polities lose touch with the Great Commission as well, but those with an episcopal polity tend to spread the effect more directly throughout their more integrated system. The Salvation Army, for example, is so well-known for its stellar relief and recovery agencies that many people, regardless of their faith, are not even aware that it is actually a church, with episcopal polity in military garb. Unfortunately, their congregations are often small and struggling; they have often not been able to make disciples among the people who they serve so generously. Anglican or Episcopal churches often focus on their liturgy or history; Pentecostal churches with episcopal polity typically focus on spiritual gifts and exuberant worship. While any denomination can elevate its distinctives above its mission, hierarchical organizations do so more systematically than others.

2) *Layers of bureaucracy in episcopal systems can easily smother missional effectiveness.* In 1969, *The Peter Principle* asserted that individuals in a

hierarchy tend to rise to their level of incompetence and stay there.[4] More than one rector and vestry have experienced the frustration of needing changes at the parish level only to face interference from a bishop lacking the inclination or the ability to support them. *The Peter Principle* would suggest that some overseers would serve better by remaining in the parish ministry where they had once demonstrated effectiveness. However, the ecclesiastical culture is often a step worse. It is common for higher levels of denominational office to be filled with individuals who never did grow large missional congregations at the local level; instead they ascended the ranks through institutional loyalty and personal connections.

3) *Denominations that relocate pastors every four or five years make it difficult for congregations to build a climate of missional accountability.* An incompetent pastor in such a system will generally be tolerated because everyone knows a change is coming in a few years. Unfortunately, those few years may be critical to the viability of the congregation's mission in its community, and the few years that follow may well repeat the pattern. On the other hand, an effective pastor in such a system may be reassigned and thus not have enough time to transform and build a congregation strong enough to survive a successor who lacks the same level of vision and experience. Whether ill-timed moves stem from lack of intentionality or from competing intentions of the congregation and the denomination, the result works against accountability.

4) *Venerable structures, whose usefulness has long since calcified into crippling rigidity, make it hard for winning innovations to emerge.* Some episcopal denominations, for example, are blessed and cursed with ostensible lifetime employment for their clergy. This apparent guarantee does not easily lend itself to serious accountability. As another example, an historic book of church order—carefully and prayerfully composed for the needs of the movement in a certain culture and era—may force contemporary congregations to make function follow form. It's a good thing that none of the original churches addressed in the New Testament have survived to the present day. Can you imagine a 2000 year-old congregation that says, "We've never done it that way before"?

This chapter was intended as an "equal opportunity offender." There is no agenda to let any of our movements off the hook for the ways that we as leaders defeat our own purpose in church ministry. Each of our tribes has ample stupidity to confront and overcome. Given the number of officials presiding over ministries in decline and the resilience of their tenure,

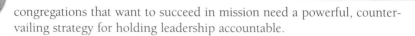

congregations that want to succeed in mission need a powerful, counter-vailing strategy for holding leadership accountable.

SUMMARY & PREVIEW

- *It's hard to win if you're not in the game (inward focus).*
- *It's hard to win if the players don't know their positions (anarchy).*
- *It's hard to win if everybody picks the plays (democracy).*
- *It's hard to win if a committee picks the plays (oligarchy).*
- *It's hard to win if bureaucrats pick the plays (hierarchy).*

The next chapter will introduce three basic elements that make any game worth playing and will apply these elements to the dynamics of a winning congregation. Finally, an overview of the Accountable Leadership strategy will bring all three elements togethe

Notes

1. http://en.wikipedia.org/wiki/Roger_Williams_(theologian) (accessed on November 15, 2005)

2. http://www.newgenevacenter.org/our-story/20_Knox.htm

3. http://www.afirstlook.com/archive/groupthink.cfm?source=archther

4. Laurence J. Peter and Raymond Hull, *The Peter Principle* (New York: William Morrow, 1969).

Three Basics Make a
Game Worth Playing

Baseball is 90% mental; the other half is physical.
Yogi Berra

THERE ARE THREE BASIC ELEMENTS THAT MAKE A GAME WORTH PLAYING: the object of the game, the rules of the game, and how to keep score. In Lewis Carroll's *Alice in Wonderland,* the Dodo organized something called a "caucus race."

> First it marked out a race-course, in a sort of circle ("the exact shape doesn't matter," it said), and then all the party were placed along the course, here and there. There was no "One, two, three, and away," but they began running when they liked, and left off when they liked, so that it was not easy to know when the race was over. However, when they had been running half-an-hour or so, and were quite dry again, the Dodo suddenly called out, "The race is over!" and they all crowded round it, panting, and asking, "But who has won?" This question the Dodo could not answer without a great deal of thought, and it sat for a long time with one finger pressed upon its forehead, (the position in which you usually see Shakespeare, in the pictures of him), while the rest waited in silence. At last the Dodo said "Everybody has won, and all must have prizes."[1]

The Dodo's race had none of the elements that make a game worth playing. There was no object, there were no rules, and no one knew how to keep score. The race was run only for the benefit of drying off the runners. Too many church-going dodos are running congregations in circles for side benefits such as personal growth, enjoying friends, feeling important, and—for some dodos—collecting paychecks. Their game is not worth playing.

The Object of the Game

Know much about Rugby? Neither do I. So I looked up the International Rugby Football Board. Here is the very first item in the Preface to *The Laws of Rugby Football:* "The Object of the Game is that two teams of fifteen players each, observing fair play according to the Laws and a sporting spirit, should by carrying, passing, kicking and grounding the ball score as many points as possible, the team scoring the greater number of points to be the winner of the match."[2] From reading that one sentence I realize I still have much to learn about the rules and how to keep score, but at least I know what those Brits in striped shirts are trying to accomplish.

The object of the game tells you why you are playing. The theological term for this purpose is *mission*. For any great contest, it is important to start with the final objective. In Stephen Covey's famous list, the second habit of highly effective people is this: "Begin with the end in mind."[3] Mission, goal, objective, outcome, result, fruit, purpose, end—all of these can be synonyms for the object of the game. There is another set of terms, however, that we do not want to confuse with the object of the game, terms such as: strategy, play, tactic, action, technique, process, activity, and means. The former describe our intended destination. The latter describe our avenues of approach. A mission-driven congregation understands that faithfulness is not complete without fruitfulness.

The Rules of the Game

A second element in any game worth playing is the rulebook. People often react negatively to the very idea of rules because rules can easily multiply to the point of oppression. In fact, contemporary expressions of innovation, creativity, and achievement include phrases like "breaking all the rules" and "coloring outside the lines." This pleasure of escaping regulations may deceive us into thinking that the game of life and the games of life would be better played without rules. But it just isn't so.

Beyond the simple necessity that rules must exist to produce the pleasure of breaking them, a short list of wise boundaries actually creates the conditions required to enjoy freedom, if not freedom itself. Jesus condensed the Mosaic Law into just two rules: "'Love the Lord your God with all your heart and with all your soul and with all your strength and with all your mind'; and, 'Love your neighbor as yourself.'" (Luke 10:27, TNIV)

Sensible boundaries are the prerequisite not only of morality, but also of emotional health, physical safety, social responsibility, and international security. Ironically, boundaries are even the prerequisite of artistic expression and creativity.

> First autumn morning:
> The mirror I stare into
> Shows my father's face.
> Murakami Kijo (1865–1938).

This poem by a Japanese master is a *haiku*. The main rule that applies to this form of poetry is simple: One line of five syllables, one line of seven syllables, and then another line of five syllables are required. Three other rules are less obvious but add to the beauty of the work: a) the poem should be cut into two separate but complementary parts with a punctuation break following either the first or second line, b) following tradition, the topic must relate to the common person, and c) each poem must contain a *kigo*, a season word, to indicate at least indirectly in which season the Haiku is set.[4] We could just as easily discuss the form of the English sonnet, Hebrew parallelism, or urban rap. While inappropriate structure stifles creativity, appropriate structure unleashes creativity. Even "free verse" follows a set of rules, albeit those of the poet's own making.

If appropriate boundaries are needed for foot races and poetry, it should come as no surprise that boundaries make an essential contribution to the success of a missional congregation. In order to play with honor and meaning, we must know the rules of the game.

How to Keep Score

Every game worth playing has a way to keep score, so that you can see who is winning during the game and who takes home the prize when it's over. Most people would not argue that there is only one right way to keep score for all kinds of games. Games are scored as a matter of convention rather than natural law. What's important is that before the game starts, the participants agree on the way points will be awarded, so there is a fair basis for calling it: win, lose, or draw. The Dodo in *Alice* had no way to keep score, so the question of who won the race had him stumped—until he dreamed up a creative solution: "Everybody has won, and all must have prizes!" But let's not miss the consequence of the Dodo's egalitarian scorecard: *the game was meaningless.*

The missional congregation is all about meaningful consequences, some of them eternal. The Dodo Protocol cannot be applied to making disciples; it's not that kind of game. We can honor neither the mission nor the pastor with a system that says, "Everybody has been effective, and all must have raises!" Without keeping score there are no real winners.

The Accountable Leadership Strategy

The Accountable Leadership strategy offered in this book brings together all three elements of the game for congregations and their pastors. The object of the game is prescribed in the form of Mission Principles. The rules of the game are called Boundary Principles, expressed as prohibitions. The way to keep score is defined through Accountability Principles. The Mission and Boundary Principles are addressed from the board to the pastor to keep the congregation's ministry both fruitful and faithful. The Accountability Principles are addressed from the board to its chairperson to keep the board's work focused and fair. Taken together, these standards for mission, boundaries, and accountability are called the Guiding Principles. They come to life through the performance of four key players, each with a unique position to play: the board playing the governance position, the pastor playing the leadership position, the staff playing the management position, and the congregation playing the ministry position.

Figure 3.1 shows the three elements of the game using the analogy of a soccer field. Representing the object of the game is the goal, a rectangular frame open at the front and cased in netting at the top, back, and sides. The object of the play is to kick the ball through the opening; the object of the game is to repeat this more often than your opponent. Each time a goal is made, a point is added to the scoreboard. If the ball is kicked over the top of the goal or to either side of it, no points are awarded because the ball is out of bounds. These boundaries are conventions determined by the commission of the sport and built to regulation. The game would not suffer much if the dimensions of the goal were a bit larger or a bit smaller, but there would be an uproar if the dimensions were changed after a game had already begun. At the bottom, the goal is bounded by the ground itself. There is no need to design a boundary of convention at this point because the players are already limited by a natural boundary.

FIGURE 3.1 Relationship of Goal, Boundaries, & Scoring

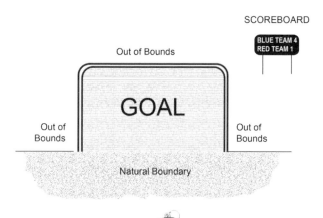

Turning from our elementary discussion of soccer, let's apply the analogy to ministry (Figure 3.2). The centerpiece is the mission of the congregation, the very reason for our existence in the community. This mission would be defined by a concise mission statement and broken down into a handful of key components. Each of those components would then serve as a category of measurable goals for the congregation. The effectiveness of the pastor's leadership would be scored through an annual review of progress toward accomplishing the goals. Therefore, the scoreboard reflects a competition of one year against another rather than one team against another. The issue is not comparing one pastor against another but measuring a pastor's performance against an agreed upon standard.

FIGURE 3.2 Analogy to Mission, Boundaries & Accountability

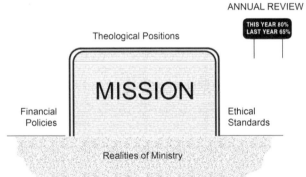

What strategies and tactics should the pastor and staff use in an effort to achieve the mission? They may use *any means they think best*—as long as they do not violate the boundaries agreed upon beforehand. Think back to our athletic metaphor. Sports commissioners and referees establish and enforce the standards, but they do not tell the teams how to play the game. A soccer team and its captain are free to run with the ball the full length and breadth of the field. They can kick the ball with the left leg or the right, and can even butt it with their heads. The officials do not tell them what to do or when to do it. The officials tell them only what *not* to do and when *not* to do it: no hands (except for the goalie), no stepping off the field, no abuse of other players, no points for balls over or to either side of the goal. The Accountable Leadership strategy applies this freedom within boundaries to pastoral leadership. The pastor is the leader and is expected to lead, not merely to submit suggestions for approval. However, there are certain boundaries stated up front, such as financial policies, theological commitments, and ethical standards. These must not be violated, but anything else is fair game. In addition, there are some natural boundaries that automatically limit the options available to the pastor. Analogous to the ground forming the base of a soccer goal, these realities of ministry include the blessing of God, the responsiveness of people, the laws of the land, and pervasive norms of culture. It is importance to understand and communicate these realities but pointless to write *rules* about them.

At this point we'll move from our depiction of the three elements of the game to a depiction of the four players that bring the game to life. Part 2 of the book will cover the three elements above in greater detail, and part 3 will cover the four players in greater detail. But for now, let's get an overview of these players.

FIGURE 3.3 Accountable Leadership Organizational Chart

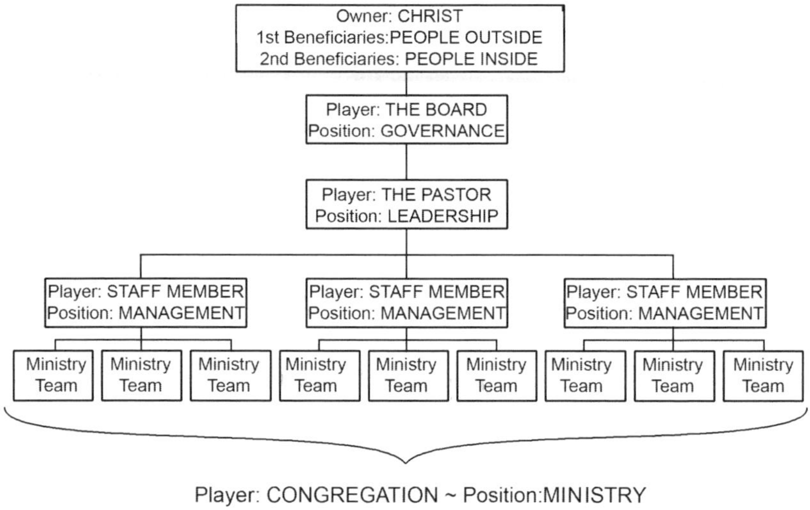

```
┌─────────────────────────────────────┐
│ Owner: CHRIST                        │
│ 1st Beneficiaries:PEOPLE OUTSIDE     │
│ 2nd Beneficiaries: PEOPLE INSIDE     │
└─────────────────────────────────────┘
        ┌──────────────────────┐
        │ Player: THE BOARD     │
        │ Position: GOVERNANCE  │
        └──────────────────────┘
        ┌──────────────────────┐
        │ Player: THE PASTOR    │
        │ Position: LEADERSHIP  │
        └──────────────────────┘
```

Player: STAFF MEMBER Position: MANAGEMENT	Player: STAFF MEMBER Position: MANAGEMENT	Player: STAFF MEMBER Position: MANAGEMENT
Ministry Team / Ministry Team / Ministry Team	Ministry Team / Ministry Team / Ministry Team	Ministry Team / Ministry Team / Ministry Team

Player: CONGREGATION ~ Position:MINISTRY

It is possible and, for accountability purposes, helpful to depict the players by using a standard organizational chart. Accountability requires a functional measure of hierarchy, regardless of polity or philosophy of ministry. In the top box of Figure 3.3, above the four players is the Owner of the organization, Christ himself, along with those whom he calls his Church to serve. Accountable to Christ (as well as to people in some manner determined by polity) is the first player, the board. The position played by the board is governance. Accountable to the board is the pastor, who plays the position of leadership. Accountable to the pastor is the staff, which plays the position of management. *Staff* in this book refers to the managers of ministries in the congregation without regard to employment or compensation status. Accountable to the staff are the various ministry teams, through which the members of congregation play the position of ministry.

While the organizational chart correctly reflects the lines of accountability, it fails to capture the functional relationship of the four players and positions. Figure 3.4 is a less conventional chart, designed to fill the gap inherent in the organizational chart. The most dominant player is the congregation itself, active in outward focused ministry. The rest of the organization is designed to empower the members. Directly underneath the congregation, supporting its ministry through equipping and coordination (also known as management), is the staff—both paid and volunteer. Out in front is the leader of the church, the pastor. The pastor leads the staff by directing it (thus the solid line) but leads the congregation primarily through teaching and the board primarily through envisioning (thus the two broken lines). The board undergirds the pastor in a similar way that the staff supports the congregation. The function of governance is to support and ensure effective pastoral leadership using the Guiding Principles.[5] Note in both Figure 3.3 and Figure 3.4 that the pastor is the only link between board and staff and the only member of both groups. This provides both a healthy connection and a healthy separation between governance by the board and management by the staff. This link of pastoral leadership creates the freedom each group needs to make its vital contribution.

FIGURE 3.4 Accountable Leadership Functional Chart

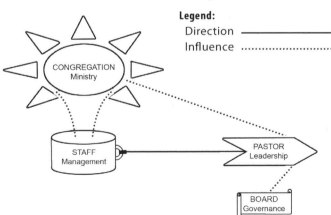

The Accountable Leadership strategy positions four major players to succeed at the mission of making disciples of Jesus Christ. The strategy takes seriously the need to prescribe mission, to prohibit crossing the boundaries, and to define the process of accountability. Object of the game, rules of the game, and how to keep score—all three are present in a meaningful contest. All three are brought together by the Accountable Leadership strategy. We don't play just to dry ourselves off, as did the Dodo and company. We play to win—on purpose.

SUMMARY & PREVIEW

- *The object of the game lets you know why you're playing.*

- *The rules of the game let you know who's cheating.*

- *The score lets you know when you're winning.*

- *The Accountable Leadership strategy puts all three basics together.*

Part 2 comes next. There we will cover in detail, for the context of congregational ministry, the elements of the game that were briefly introduced in this chapter: mission, boundaries, and accountability. First up is mission, in a chapter entitled, "The Object of the Game Defines Responsibility."

Notes

1. Lewis Carroll, *Alice's Adventures in Wonderland,* (New York: William Morrow, 1866), 33-34.

2. http://www.uidaho.edu/clubs/womens_rugby/RugbyRoot/rugby/Rules/LawBook/preface.html#object (accessed on 11-24-04)

3. Stephen R. Covey, *The 7 Habits of Highly Effective People* (New York: Simon & Schuster, 1989), 95–144.

4. http://www.toyomasu.com/haiku/

5. Accountable Leadership is a distinct alternative to John Carver's Policy Governance model, Tom Bandy's *Christian Chaos* model, or a traditional management model. Overlaps and influences on any number of tactical details exist among them, but the strategic premise of any one of these four models is incompatible with each of the others.

PART TWO

DO WE UNDERSTAND
THE GAME?

CHAPTER FOUR

The Object of the Game Defines Responsibility

We succeed only as we identify in life, or in war, or in anything else, a single overriding objective, and make all other considerations bend to that one objective.
Dwight D. Eisenhower

WHILE TRAVELING IN EUROPE WITH MY FAMILY, I spotted the perfect souvenir for my colleague, Paul Borden. It was a pack of cigarettes from a convenience store in Germany. Paul is not a smoker, but I knew he would enjoy this gift anyway. Why? Because the brand name read, BALANCE, followed by the warning: *Dieses tötet Sie* ("This will kill you"). For years I have heard Paul caution ministry leaders that simply maintaining balance in light of biblical urgencies and cultural challenges is lethal to the health and growth of congregations. Now he has a memorable teaching aid.

If the Church is to be missional rather than institutional, we must begin with a clear understanding of what that mission is. In *Surfing the Edge of Chaos,* Pascale, Millemann, and Gioja assert, "equilibrium is death," as the first principle necessary for adaptive leadership.[1] Jim Collins promotes the hedgehog concept as a metaphor for the importance of a single unifying idea.[2] Buckingham and Clifton developed the StrengthsFinder profile to help people zero in on their unique contribution.[3] The common element of these recent works is the same concept expressed to me in college by a karate teacher from Indonesia, in these memorable words: "Waann . . . you . . . punch—must *focus!*"

For the local Christian congregation, what is the single overriding objective to which all other considerations must be bent? This chapter will propose and defend an unequivocal answer to that question.

The Source of Our Objective

Where are we to look for a legitimate definition of our overriding objective, our purpose? If the congregation were a public corporation, we would look to its members or their representatives to define the purpose of the enterprise because as shareholders, they would be the owners. If the congregation were a small Mom and Pop business, we would look to the family matriarch and patriarch to define the purpose because as sole proprietors, they would be the owners. Though the course of many smaller congregations is controlled by one of these two models by default, we know theologically that the Church is not owned by its members or by a dominant family among its members. The New Testament leaves no doubt about who owns the Church: "And he [Christ] is the head of the body, the church; he is the beginning and the firstborn from among the dead, so that in everything he might have the supremacy." (Colossians 1:18, TNIV) Jesus Christ is the Head of the Church, the Lord of the Church. When it comes time to vote on the mission of our local congregation, Christ casts the only ballot that counts.

Since Jesus Christ is the owner of his Church and thus all of its local expressions, we do not get to dream up the mission for our congregation. The Lord of the Church is the one who has "all authority in heaven and on earth" to give us our marching orders. Defining the mission of our congregation is not an exercise in creativity but an exercise in discernment. So, in order to anchor this critical definition in the words of Christ himself, we will focus our attention next on the final instructions Jesus left his disciples in Matthew 28:19–20 and reflect on their relationship to other mission-related statements Jesus made during his earthly ministry.

Jesus's Final Word on the Matter

Since at least the time of Justinian von Welz (1621–68), Dutch missionary to modern-day Surinam, the final instructions of the risen Christ to his disciples have been aptly called the "Great Commission."[4] This descriptor seems all the more fitting in contrast to the limited commission Jesus had previously given the twelve when he sent them on a training assignment to preach only to the "lost sheep of Israel."[5] However, the commission in Matthew 28 deserves the adjective *great* not only for the breadth of its beneficiaries but also for the tone, the structure, and the timing of its delivery:

> When they saw him, they worshiped him; but some doubted. Then Jesus came to them and said, "All authority in heaven and on earth has been given to me. Therefore go and make disciples of all nations, baptizing them in the name of the Father and of the Son and of the Holy Spirit, and teaching them to obey everything I have commanded you. And surely I am with you always, to the very end of the age." (Matthew 28:17–20, TNIV)

The emotional tone of Jesus's words at the end of Matthew's Gospel is both sobering and reassuring. The disciples' faith had been restored and deepened following the Resurrection, but according to verse 17, some of the eleven were still plagued with doubts. Jesus begins his words not with the imperative itself but with the announcement of a new cosmic reality that undergirds it: "All authority in heaven and on earth has been given to me." He concludes with a solemn promise of his own abiding presence with those who obey his commission. It is difficult to imagine how the directive that is sandwiched between this announcement and this promise could be given more weight in the emphasis of the text and in the experience of the disciples.

The structure of Jesus's command is comprehensive and deliberate. Figure 4.1 depicts the relationship of the Greek clauses in translation. Four verbs shape the backbone of the syntax. Only one, "make disciples" *(mateusthete)* is in the imperative mood and anchors the main clause of the sentence. The other three verbs appear in the form of participles and create three subordinate clauses in support of the main verb. Each of the participles takes on an imperatival force because of its association with the main verb in the imperative. This force is most evident for "going" *(poreuthentes)* because it precedes "make disciples."[6] The participles that follow—"baptizing" *(baptizontes)* and "teaching" *(didaskontes)*—complete the picture of actions that accompany making disciples. The process begins with proactive outreach to the various cultures (going), leads to public identification with Christ and his people (baptizing), and culminates in teaching obedience to the commands of Jesus, including of course his ultimate mandate here: to produce more disciples.

FIGURE 4.1 Syntactical Structure of the Great Commission

Going,

Make disciples of all nations,

Baptizing them in the name of the Father, of the Son, and of the Holy Spirit, and

Teaching them to obey everything I have commanded you.

Panta ta ethne (all the nations), in the accusative case, functions as the object of the verb *matheteusate* (make disciples), which is normally an intransitive verb, but in this instance takes an object. The theological significance of this construction is that **the core of Jesus's command is to produce new, committed followers from the raw material of the nations,** i.e. people of every ethnicity. As distinguished missiologist David Hesselgrave observes,

> There is a widespread misunderstanding as to what 'discipling' might be. It is not just introducing people to Christ as some seem to think. Nor is it taking the most promising converts and making good, solid Christians out of them as very many seem to think. No, 'disciple' is an inclusive word. To disciple means to make followers, students, learners. To understand it we simply need to follow Christ and his disciples along the path that led to Calvary. To understand it we simply need to accompany early Christians in Acts as they lived out their faith in the midst of difficulties and propagated it in the face of opposition. Discipleship begins when people respond to God's Word in repentance and faith. It continues in company with other believers in the church of Jesus Christ. And it ends in the glory of God's heaven.[7]

In addition to the tone and the structure of Matthew 28:19–20, the timing of Jesus's instructions, perhaps most importantly, marks off the Great Commission as truly great. Parting words, especially from someone important to us who we will never see again, carry a deep significance in universal human experience. Because of Jesus's death, resurrection, and pending ascension, his parting words carried a cosmic weight that defies comparison. And those parting words define the objective of his Church until the end of the age: to reproduce the spiritual life Jesus himself had breathed into her.

No one could accuse Jesus of surprising his disciples with the evangelistic nature of this objective. From the original calling of the first disciples, Simon Peter and Andrew, Jesus made it clear that multiplication would be the goal of their discipleship. " 'Come, follow me,' Jesus said, 'and I will send you out to fish for people.' " (Matt. 4:19, TNIV) So the first thing the original disciples heard about the nature of their calling was also the last thing they heard about the nature of their commission. Just as Jesus had sought them out and invited them to follow him, they were to seek out others and invite them to join in the same type of relationship.

Jesus's Earlier Mission Statements

The Great Commission was certainly not the first comment on the purpose of ministry that Jesus had made. We have already mentioned the call of the first disciples and the limited commission to preach to the "lost sheep of Israel." Both of these prepared the disciples for Jesus's ultimate mandate. Table 4.1 contains representative examples of mission statements made by Jesus during his earthly ministry and recorded in the Gospels. Each statement carries a nuance of its own yet supports, rather than displaces, the redemptive nature of the Great Commission.

TABLE 4.1 Earlier Mission Statements of Jesus

REFERENCE	PHRASE	THEME
Matt. 5:17	not to abolish but to fulfill [Scripture]	Continuity with OT
Matt. 9:13	not to call the righteous, but sinners	Need for salvation
Matt. 10:34	not come to bring peace, but a sword	Acceptance vs. rejection
Mark 10:45	to serve, and to give his life as a ransom	Sacrifice vs. self-promotion
Luke 4:18–19	to proclaim the year of the Lord's favor	Deliverance by the Messiah
Luke 19:10	to seek and to save what was lost	Favor to the out of favor
John 3:17	to save the world through him	Salvation vs. condemnation
John 6:38-40	to do the will of him who sent me	Losing none who come
John 10:10	that they may have life . . . to the full.	Giving life, not stealing it

Though not found in the context of a mission statement, there are two other summary statements worthy of comparing with Jesus's final commission to the disciples because they are sometimes cited to divert attention from the Great Commission onto other priorities. One is Jesus's restatement of the Old Testament's Great Commandment, found in Matthew 22:34–40. The other is the standard used for the judgment of the nations that Jesus predicted in the Olivet Discourse, found in Matthew 24–25.

The occasion for Jesus's remarks in Matthew 22:34–40 on "the first and greatest commandment" was not an announcement of his mission or an instruction to his disciples. It was a response to the Pharisees who were testing him. Perhaps they expected him to elevate one of the Ten Commandments above the rest and open himself to criticism for neglect of the others. Instead, Jesus quoted Deuteronomy 6:5 to declare that an intimate, all-consuming relationship with God lies at the heart of all his commands. He then added, from Leviticus 19:18, that closely associated with loving God is loving those who God loves, i.e. the people around us. After deflecting the Pharisees' agenda, Jesus posed an exegetical question of his own to confront them with the divine nature of the Messiah. It left them speechless.

Those who would reinterpret the Great Commandment as some kind of competitor to the Great Commission face an uphill battle. First of all, unlike Matthew 28, Jesus's answer to the Pharisees in Matthew 22 is not intentionally framed as a statement of mission for himself or his disciples. Second, there is no conflict between the two mandates in terms of their content. And third, because Jesus emphasized that one cannot claim to love God without obeying God, it is impossible to fulfill the Great Commandment without placing the highest priority on his final and explicit instructions. To love God is to further his mission of redemption. To love our neighbors as ourselves is to share with them the life and love that we ourselves have found in Christ alone.[8]

At the end of the Olivet Discourse in Matthew 24–25, Jesus forecasts a coming judgment on the nations. The blessed are separated from the cursed on the basis of how they treated "the least of these." Some have begun to refer to this passage as the Great Criterion, perhaps to imply that the Great Commission is not an adequate statement of Christian mission. Compassion for the vulnerable is presented as an evidence of righteousness in Matthew 25. However, there is not one criterion for judgment presented here but rather *three* criteria in parallel images: wisdom, illustrated by the ten virgins (vv. 1–13); productivity, illustrated by the talents (vv. 14–30); and compassion, illustrated by the sheep and goats (vv. 31–46). The criteria of compassion, wisdom, and productivity, fall within the "everything I have commanded you" portion of Jesus's commission to the disciples. It may not legitimately be recast as an alternative to his explicit imperative to make disciples.

The Acts of the (Commissioned) Apostles

The obedience of the apostles to the commission they had received is reflected in the book of Acts. This chronicle is the self-designated sequel to the Gospel of Luke and is addressed to the same Theophilus, who may have sponsored Luke's painstaking research. Consider the "object of the game" as it was played out in the early triumphs of the church: "Day after day, in the temple courts and from house to house, they never stopped teaching and proclaiming the good news that Jesus is the Messiah." (Acts 5:42, TNIV) Up until the imprisonment of Paul, every so often the book of Acts is punctuated by a kind of update on the scoreboard. Each of these includes qualitative essentials, but the emphasis is on the quantitative growth of the disciples.

Those who accepted his message were baptized, and **about three thousand were added to their number that day**...And the Lord added to their number daily those who were being saved. *(Acts 2:41, 47, TNIV)*

But many of those who heard the word believed; and **they numbered about five thousand.** *(Acts 4:4, NRSV)*

So the word of God spread. **The number of disciples in Jerusalem increased rapidly,** and **a large number of priests** became obedient to the faith. *(Acts 6:7, TNIV)*

Then the church throughout Judea, Galilee and Samaria enjoyed a time of peace and was strengthened. Living in the fear of the Lord and encouraged by the Holy Spirit, **it increased in numbers.** *(Acts 9:31, TNIV)*

The Lord's hand was with them, and **a great number of people believed** . . . and **a great number of people were brought to the Lord.** (Acts 11: 21–24, TNIV)

But the word of God **continued to increase and spread.** *(Acts 12:24, TNIV)*

The **word of the Lord spread** through the whole region. *(Acts 13:49, TNIV)*

At Iconium Paul and Barnabas...spoke so effectively that **a great number of Jews and Greeks believed.** *(Acts 14:1, TNIV)*

They preached the good news in that city [Derbe] and **won a large number of disciples.** *(Acts 14:21, TNIV)*

So the churches were strengthened in the faith and **grew daily in numbers.** *(Acts 16:5, TNIV)*

Some of the Jews were persuaded and joined Paul and Silas, as did a **large number of God-fearing Greeks** and **not a few prominent women.** *(Acts 17:4, TNIV)*

Many of them believed, as did also a number of prominent Greek women and many Greek men [in Berea]. (Acts 17:12, TNIV)

Some of the people became followers of Paul and believed. Among them was Dionysius, a member of the Areopagus, also a woman named Damaris, and a number of others. (Acts 17:34, TNIV)

Crispus, the synagogue leader, and his entire household believed in the Lord; and many of the Corinthians who heard Paul believed and were baptized. One night the Lord spoke to Paul in a vision: "Do not be afraid; keep on speaking, do not be silent. For I am with you, and no one is going to attack and harm you, because I have many people in this city." (Acts 18:8–10, TNIV)

Many of those who believed now came and openly confessed what they had done. A number who had practiced sorcery brought their scrolls together and burned them publicly. When they calculated the value of the scrolls, the total came to fifty thousand drachmas. In this way the word of the Lord spread widely and grew in power. (Acts 19:18–20, TNIV)

Even after Paul was arrested and transported to Rome, he kept winning people to Christ: "For two whole years Paul stayed there in his own rented house and welcomed all who came to see him. He proclaimed the kingdom of God and taught about the Lord Jesus Christ—with all boldness and without hindrance!" (Acts 28:30–31, TNIV)

Winning at the Object of the Game

There is a difference between a win and a play. Plays exist for wins, not the other way around. The purpose of a play is to score. If a team does not score goals, it makes no difference how well or how cleverly they are able to execute plays. By not scoring goals, the team has ultimately failed. Kobe Bryant and Shaquille O'Neal both joined the Los Angeles Lakers basketball team in the 1996–97 season.[9] For the first three years, each of them played brilliantly. For the first three years, the team did not win a championship. Not until coach Phil Jackson got the two superstars to focus on wins for the team instead of on their individual plays did the Lakers begin to top the Western Conference of the NBA.

One reason that job descriptions for church staff have limited value is that they emphasize plays over wins. At the top comes a short statement to describe the general purpose of the position. Next comes a clarification of who reports to whom. The rest is given to activities: The employee will cover certain areas, oversee certain areas, put so many hours into certain activities, and so on. The description concludes with our favorite part:

compensation and benefits, which are linked to activity but not productivity. The truth is that leading groups, meeting for worship, attending concerts, teaching classes, preaching sermons, counseling couples, cleaning neighborhoods, and all the other good plays a congregation may execute only prevail if they make more disciples.

When it comes to the church, the object of the game is to make disciples from the raw human material of every ethnicity. The object is not to find them, gather them, or improve them. The object is to make them. A disciple *(mathetes)*, is a learner—not a spiritual giant. The Twelve were called disciples from the first day they began to follow Jesus. The Great Commission is all about the inflow of people beginning their relationship with Christ, passing from death to life. The stakes of this mandate don't call for balance but for passion.

SUMMARY & PREVIEW

- *Jesus is the final authority on the object of the game for his disciples.*

- *The Great Commission is Jesus's final word on the matter.*

- *Acts is a story of the Great Commission in progress—measurable progress.*

- *Church activities are the plays; more disciples are the wins that justify the plays.*

The object of the game gets us started, but if that is all we use for decisions, we might think the end justifies the means. To avoid that pitfall, we need to know the rules of the game as well as the object. Chapter 5 is all about how the right use of boundaries can authorize freedom that is safe and effective."

Notes

1. Richard T. Pascale, Mark Millemann, and Linda Gioja, *Surfing the Edge of Chaos: The Laws of Nature and the New Laws of Business*, (New York: Three Rivers Press, 2000), 19–41.

2. Jim Collins, *Good to Great: Why Some Companies Make the Leap...and Others Don't*, (New York: Harper Business, 2001), 90–119.

3. Marcus Buckingham and Donald O. Clifton, *Now Discover Your Strengths*, (New York: Free Press, 2001), 8.

4. http://home.snu.edu/~hculbert/slogans.htm. See also Hesselgrave, "As is well known, many Reformers held to the position that the Great Commission was given to, and fulfilled by, the apostles. The Spirit used men like Justinian von Welz, Phillip Spener, and William Carey to impress upon the church the fact that

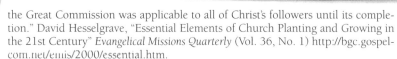

the Great Commission was applicable to all of Christ's followers until its completion." David Hesselgrave, "Essential Elements of Church Planting and Growing in the 21st Century" *Evangelical Missions Quarterly* (Vol. 36, No. 1) http://bgc.gospelcom.net/emis/2000/essential.htm.

5. Matthew 10:5–6

6. D. A. Carson, "Matthew," in *Expositor's Bible Commentary,* ed. Frank Gaebelein, vol. 8 (Grand Rapids: Zondervan, 1984), pp. 594-599.

7. Hesselgrave, http://bgc.gospelcom.net/emis/2000/essential.htm—Copyright © 2000 Evangelism and Missions Information Service. This article originally appeared in the January, 2000 issue of EMQ. All rights reserved.

8. Lyle Schaller compares "first commandment churches" and "second commandment churches," not as competitors but as complementary ministries with an emphasis on one commandment or the other in *Small Congregation, Big Potential: Ministry in the Small Membership Church,* (Nashville: Abingdon, 2003).

9. Bill Harris, "Kobe, Shaq Work It Out: Lakers' 1-2 Punch a Perfect Combo," *Toronto Sun,* June 11, 2002. There is no difference between professional and amateur games in this analogy or any other analogy in this book. The issue is a commitment to results, not whether money is involved.

CHAPTER FIVE
The Rules of the Game Create Authority

"A few strong instincts and a few plain rules suffice us."
Ralph Waldo Emerson

IN THE DAYS OF THE SOVIET UNION what was the difference between taking a road trip in Russia and a road trip in Nebraska? For either one you would have needed an automobile, fuel, and a driver. But in Russia you would need one thing more that you would not need in Nebraska: permission. Travel in a totalitarian state is based on approval. Travel in a free country is based on authorization—as long as you operate the vehicle within a few simple traffic laws, you are free to drive wherever you need to go.

Leading a ministry in many local churches is like taking a road trip in the Soviet Union: you may not be surrounded by Communists, but it's hard to get the resources, it's hard to get permission, and it's hard not to feel that you're stuck in a previous century. And yet the proper use of a few clear boundaries can create the freedom and authority that ministry leaders need to accomplish the mission of the church.

A Word of Warning about Rules

Some of us love rules. Some of us love to break them. Either instinct is likely to hurt people without a proper understanding of both the value and limitations of creating boundaries for behavior.

Earlier we identified the elements that make a game worth playing: the object of the game, the rules of the game, and how to keep score. At this point it is critical to emphasize that *keeping the rules is not the object of the game.* The object of the game for a congregation is the Great Commission: making disciples of Jesus Christ. Keeping the rules is simply a way to focus the power necessary to achieve the object of the game. It is possible to keep all of the rules and still lose the game. It happens all the time in sporting events by design—there are winners and losers. It happens all the time in congregations by default—we're on the winning side, but we think and act like losers. If we confuse the rules of the game with the object of the game, we may wind up defining success as doing church without making mistakes, even if we are not making any new disciples. There are two distortions of the Accountable

Leadership strategy that merit a strong warning at this point: one is a warning to and about pastors; the other is a warning to and about boards.

In the course of training and consulting with congregations, I have encountered pastors who are attracted to a system that gives them great freedom and authority as a leader, but who are not interested in using that leadership for mission, at least not the Great Commission. Instead, they see an increase in their authority as a means to some other end. This authority may become a means to promote a theological or spiritual agenda among believers, in which case the church is not making disciples but simply gathering existing disciples and giving them a makeover. This authority may become a means to advance a political agenda in the community, in which case the church is not making disciples but simply harvesting the resources of disciples for use in some other cause. Sadly, this authority may become a means to protect a job, in which case the church is not making disciples but merely servicing disciples in a way that creates personal security for the pastor.

The antidote for pastoral abuse of authority is one-part mission and one-part accountability. When the object of the game (mission) is clearly defined as making disciples, and the way to keep score (accountability) is based on an increase in the number of new disciples made, the pastor's authority is used in servant-leadership to the cause of Christ rather than diverted to some other purpose.

At this point, the warning to and about church boards has more to do with the multiplication of rules than about their abuse. I have seen church board members who latch on to parts of the Accountable Leadership strategy as a means to *control* their pastor rather than to *empower* their pastor. They hear about accountability and guiding principles and begin to have visions of tying a string to each joint of their "leader," all running back to the board as spiritual puppeteer.

To counter the temptation of a board to control its pastor, here are two simple disciplines to practice: 1) Spend more time on discussing the desired outcomes to achieve (mission) than on the undesired activities to avoid (boundaries). 2) Keep organizational documents short and to the point, especially with regard to boundary statements.

As we approach the function of boundaries in the Accountable Leadership strategy, both pastors and boards in local congregations are cautioned to remember that keeping the rules—while important for authorizing acceptable activities—is not the object of the game. Jesus commissioned his Church to make disciples of all nations, not to make decisions on all notions.

How Boundaries Work

Simply put, boundaries tell you how not to play the game. The rule-book is not a play-book. It is fundamentally a set of prohibitions, not prescriptions. While prohibitions sound somewhat negative in tone and appear entirely negative in form, they actually create a most positive freedom of movement when properly understood and applied.

The significance of this dynamic relationship between boundaries and authority must not be missed. Tom Bandy calls it *proscriptive thinking* in his book on reinventing congregations, *Christian Chaos.* "Proscriptive thinking requires the board to think *negatively* in order to empower mission *positively.*"[1] John Carver refers to it as *proactive constraint* in his book, *Boards That Make a Difference,* aimed at nonprofit organizations. "The board has neither the time nor the expertise to state everything that should be done. It does have the sense of values necessary to recognize what should not be done. The principle is simple and, perhaps more than any other principle, enables excellence in governing."[2] For biblical precedent, we might cite Jesus's words "Whoever is not against us is for us,"[3] or the language of "thou shalt not" in the Mosaic Law. But the first use of boundaries to create freedom goes back much further.

The first rule in human history was a boundary designed to create freedom. Soon after Adam's creation, God said to him, "You are free to eat from any tree in the garden; but you must not eat from the tree of the knowledge of good and evil, for when you eat of it you will surely die."[4] By defining one simple boundary, God authorized the first humans to choose any fruit they wished, except for one. If Adam had later requested a meeting to seek permission to eat fruit salad for lunch, his Creator would not have bothered to show up. Instead, he would have sent an angel—not an important angel like Michael or Gabriel, but a rookie like Clarence.[5] The angel would not be sent to rule on the menu request but to reprimand Adam: "Why are you troubling the Lord with a request about fruit salad? He already told you that you could eat anything you want, except for fruit from that tree over there. See the big red circle with the diagonal slash? That's all you need to watch out for. Otherwise you are free to choose anything in garden."

God did not issue the first prohibition to oppress Adam and Eve but to empower them with an abundance of freedom and resources to fulfill his purpose for them. A few simple, well-placed boundaries in the congregation can provide the pastor and staff with an abundance of freedom and resources to fulfill Christ's purpose for his people.

Fair Game

One implication of proscriptive thinking is that anything within the rules is fair game. That, of course, does not mean that any activity within the rules will win the game, just that it is one of many acceptable alternatives from which to choose as a leader attempts to construct a winning strategy.

Let's return to the illustration of a soccer field used in chapter 3 to illustrate three basic elements of a game. In Figure 3.1 (on page 44), adjacent to the goal and not far from the scoreboard are certain areas of the field that are designated as out of bounds. How are these designations made? In some places there is no need for an explicit boundary designation because of natural boundaries. The firm surface of the playing field prevents the ball from going under the goal, so there is no need to write a rule about it. In other places, the boundaries are marked off by devices such as painted lines or the frame of the goal. If a player steps over the line or kicks the ball outside the frame, the referees can easily judge what is out of bounds and what is fair play.

To focus our attention more keenly on boundaries, consider Figure 5.1 as the top view of a soccer field. Ignoring for now the internal markers such as the goal area, penalty area and centerline, in broad terms we see that the "touchline" (boundary) on either side of the field creates great freedom of movement for the players. By defining only what is not allowed, these boundaries automatically authorize any area within them as fair game. There is no need for specific approvals from the referees. In fact, seeking specific approvals for plays would be childish, distracting, and self-defeating. Though the boards and bylaws of plateaued and declining congregations routinely restrict their top leaders and players to a system of specific approvals, there is a better way: To win on purpose, use boundaries as a tool to preauthorize any and all means that are ethical and prudent.

FIGURE 5.1 Boundaries And Freedom

For example, let's say a church needs a new computer system. In a specific approval system, the office administrator, who understands the needs and solutions far better than anyone else in the organization, would have to prepare a proposal for the pastor to take to a board meeting. The pastor would love to empower the administrator simply to act decisively and not waste time writing up a proposal, but the board requires the pastor to bring all expenditures over $5,000 for approval. The next meeting is three weeks away. When the board finally meets, it gives the proposal fifteen minutes of consideration. One of the board members has a cousin in the computer business and thinks that a ByteMaster-3000 is definitely the way to go. A former missionary on the board thinks the money would be better spent on relief efforts in the Murky Isles. The rest of the members are worn out from the debates on carpet and youth camp they have endured after a long day at work. Ultimately, the board postpones the discussion for the next meeting. By the time the proposal gets approved, the computer market has changed, the office backlog has tripled, and the office administrator is quietly circulating resumes.

Now, what if the board used boundaries instead of approvals? The administrator tells the pastor about the need and suggests a way to solve it. The pastor verifies that funds are available without dipping below the minimum reserve required by the board (a boundary) and tells the administrator to use good judgment, get competitive bids (a boundary), and work within $7,500 (a boundary). The capable administrator finds a great one-time deal on eBay for a $15,000 system at $6,800, clicks the mouse, and installs the new system the following week. To celebrate, the administrator takes a good friend to lunch and brags about the church. The friend is so impressed that she becomes a Christian, joins the congregation, and pays off its mortgage from a recent inheritance—well, maybe I'm stretching it a bit at this point. But you get the idea.

A governing board can create and enforce guiding principles that not only define the outcomes desired from pastoral leadership but also set the boundaries of acceptable means to pursue those outcomes. In no way does a healthy governing board shirk its responsibility to ensure God-honoring activities in the ministry of the congregation. However, instead of using the debilitating tool of specific approvals, it applies the empowering tool of simple boundaries. Instead of prescribing what can be done, it proscribes what cannot be done. So a lot more good actually gets done.

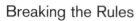

Breaking the Rules

What happens when you step over a boundary? That should depend on the boundary. Consequences in life can range all the way from warnings and fines to exile and execution. Not all of these options are available to congregations (though we may be tempted at times). Let the punishment fit the crime. If something less than a crime is involved, then something less than a punishment is appropriate as well. The particular boundaries and their relative importance is up to the collective judgment of the board. For the sake of discussion, refer to Table 5.1 as a range of options for boards to impose on a pastor or for a pastor to impose on a staff person when a boundary is being violated.

TABLE 5.1 Responses to Lack of Compliance

	INITIAL INSTANCES	CONTINUING PATTERN	STUBBORN PERSISTENCE
MINOR LAPSE	Allow room for self-correction.	Ask for corrective action.	Adjust conditions to counteract.
REAL PROBLEM	Ask for corrective action.	Impose corrective action with deadlines and penalties.	Remove from position.
SERIOUS OFFENSE	Relieve of duty and offer rehabilitation.	Remove from position.	*Never allow it to get this far.*

Here is an example of a written boundary concerning financial audits in the current Guiding Principles of the American Baptist Churches of the West: "The executive minister shall not receive, process, or disburse funds under controls that are insufficient to meet the board-appointed auditor's standards." Each year the financial records are audited, and each year the auditor provides the board with a report on their compliance with standard accounting practices. Because of the scope and complexity of ministries in the ABCW, there are frequently improvements recommended by the auditor. When these minor lapses are first noted, the board does nothing because it assumes that the executive minister will have the staff make the changes. If the same issues are cited repeatedly without improvement, the board asks the executive minister to make sure the issues are addressed. If these minor but legitimate issues remain out of compliance after a clear request for correction, the board directly revises the system in some way to eliminate or minimize any ill effects. If the lack of compliance is minor by nature, however, it never results in severe consequences.

But what if the lack of compliance is more significant? Here, for instance, is a boundary principle with higher stakes that a number of congregations using the Accountable Leadership strategy have incorporated into their Guiding Principles document: "With regard to teaching and leadership the senior pastor shall not fail to uphold high standards of biblical teaching and morality."

Let's say that the pastor and the board learn that a small group leader is distributing books and recordings that clearly contradict the basic teachings of Christianity. This is a "real problem." The pastor should ask the staff person overseeing small groups to correct the problem. If it continues, the pastor should establish a corrective plan with deadlines and penalties for the staff person. If the staff member stubbornly resists taking care of the problem, he or she should be replaced. And if the pastor does not see to the correction of this real problem, then the board should follow the same escalating response toward the pastor.

Now let's consider a more serious offense of the same boundary principle. The senior pastor's spouse discovers that the pastor is having an affair with a counselee. After confronting the pastor to no avail, the spouse asks the board to intervene. The board meets separately and jointly with each of the persons directly concerned and concludes that the pastor has indeed fallen into a moral failure. Effective immediately, the board arranges for an interim pastor with the help of the denomination and offers to the pastor a course of professional counseling and eventual restoration of ministry conditioned on submitting to their spiritual discipline. A pastor who agrees and follows through is restored, if possible, or else assisted in finding an appropriate new situation. A pastor who does not is dismissed.

The bottom line is simply this: breaking the rules results in a penalty—the higher the stakes, the steeper the cost. Does it follow that compliance with the rules is rewarded? Yes, but not in the same form that missional results are rewarded, that is to say, not with compensation or job security.

Compliance is a requisite that is rewarded in the same way that law-abiding is rewarded in society: with freedom, respect, and the opportunity to achieve something more.

Changing the Rules

The rules of a game need to be fairly stable in order for the game to be worth playing. However, at times the rules change. Our core values, of course, should not change, unless we become convinced before God that we have been wrong about something important. But lesser boundaries may need to be adjusted on the basis of experience or changing circumstances. When it's time to change the rules, the change must be decided, shaped, and applied with integrity.

To decide a change of boundaries with integrity requires that the decision be made at the legitimate level. For example, the bylaws are a congregational document; amendments at that level generally require the consent of the membership. The Guiding Principles in a church using the *Winning on Purpose* model are a board document; the congregation does not participate in approving or revising them. The pastor may produce staff-level policies at will without the approval of the board or the congregation. To mess around in each other's sandbox, so to speak, would violate the integrity of the process.

Changes in the rules must also be shaped and applied with integrity. Boundaries should not be constructed to restrict ministry leaders but to empower and protect them. If an activity is not illegal, unethical, imprudent, or unbiblical, the board has no legitimate interest in forbidding it to the staff and the people working with them in ministry.

When a new boundary truly is needed—in order to empower and protect the leader's authority to achieve the mission, it is important that the new standard be applied only to future behavior. No fair changing the rules for a game already played!

If you want your congregation to win on purpose, create ample authority for its leader through a few simple rules. In some cases, exceptionally resourceful pastors are able to lead congregations with a burdensome approval system to grow and thrive. But it's about as likely as taking a road trip in the Soviet Union. And watch out—most leaders resourceful enough to pull it off are also resourceful enough to wrangle a visa to Nebraska where they can drive a Corvette.

SUMMARY & PREVIEW

- *Keeping the rules is not the object of the game.*

- *Boundaries tell you how not to play.*

- *Anything within the rules is fair game.*

- *Breaking the rules gets you a penalty.*

- *Sometimes the rules change.*

Many congregations are afraid to trust their leaders with the authority they need to fulfill the responsibility of mission. The element of the game they don't understand is accountability. We'll see how that works next in chapter 6, "Accountability is How We Keep Score."

Notes

1. Thomas G. Bandy, *Christian Chaos: Revolutionizing the Congregation,* (Nashville: Abingdon, 1999), 63. Italics his. Bandy uses proscriptive thinking as a principle for widespread use by congregational teams, whereas its use in Accountable Leadership or in Policy Governance is targeted specifically to the authorization of means for the primary leader.

2. John Carver, *Boards That Make a Difference: A New Design for Leadership in Nonprofit and Public Organizations, 2nd ed.,* (San Francisco: Jossey-Bass, 1997), 79. For those comparing Accountable Leadership with Policy Governance, this chapter on the rules of the game covers the same ground as Carver's "limitations on executive means." This chapter does not relate to the other three of his four policy areas.

3. Mark 9:40 (TNIV). On another occasion, recorded in Matthew 12:30, Jesus said very nearly the opposite. The quotation is not given to show that proscriptive thinking is the only legitimate alternative, merely that it is not new or unbiblical.

4. Genesis 2:16–17

5. Clarence was an "Angel—Second Class," who had not yet earned his wings in Frank Capra's 1946 film, "It's a Wonderful Life."

CHAPTER SIX

Accountability is How We Keep Score

If it doesn't matter who wins or loses, then why do they keep score?
Vince Lombardi

OLYMPIC MEDALS, OPEN ELECTIONS, AND BOX OFFICE RETURNS all have one thing in common: they create a day of reckoning for human enterprise. Who will get the gold? Who will govern the country? Who will make a profit? In a healthy system, the double-edged sword of accountability cuts through good intentions, glides beyond best efforts, and lodges at the point of outcomes and consequences. The athletic world, the political scene, and the film industry each have mechanisms that say either "You did it!" or else "Not this time."

That is not to say these mechanisms function perfectly. Yet when they fail, often they trigger consequences that go beyond the conventions of accountability. There is even accountability for the failure to apply accountability: As Abraham Lincoln said, "Elections belong to the people. It is their decision. If they decide to turn their back on the fire and burn their behinds, then they will just have to sit on their blisters." We'll return to the topic of natural consequences toward the end of this chapter, but first let's explore how to build accountability into a winning congregation—on purpose.

Safe and Effective Organization

The Church exists for mission, not for structure. Nevertheless, structure is critical for long-term success because it helps or hinders effective leadership. Earlier we explored the question of mission. After staking out a position that mission should be primarily outward in focus, I raised the inherent limitations of mission and vision statements: "What, then, is the factor separating mission *articulated* from mission *accomplished*? That critical factor is the organizational culture of the congregation, which is woven from its deepest values—not some list of 'core values' on display in the foyer but the real and rarely admitted priorities that determine how money, time, and attention is distributed." This critical force of organizational culture is rooted in values but shows up through structure. A budget is a form of structure. A calendar is a form of structure. A facility—as in the story of the broken window—is a form of structure. Structure is simply the design and arrangement of tangible factors in time and space. The kind of structure *Winning on Purpose* addresses is the organizational structure of a congregation, which I define as *the arrangement of responsibility, authority, and accountability in leadership and ministry.*

TABLE 6.1 Three Real-World Structures of Church Government

	BUREAUCRATIC STRUCTURE	AUTHORITARIAN STRUCTURE	ACCOUNTABLE STRUCTURE
FORMULA	Responsibility - Authority	Responsibility + Authority	Responsibility + Authority + Accountability
RESULT	= "Safe" *but not* Effective	= "Effective" *but not* Safe	= Safe *and* Effective
METAPHOR	Placebo	Narcotic	Medicine
PASTOR AS	Employee	Dictator	Leader

Without regard to historical church polities (which will be treated in chapter 14), here in Table 6.1 are three ways that congregations arrange the three factors of responsibility, authority, and accountability in the real world of church government. The U.S. Food and Drug Administration enforces two criteria for approval of a new medicine: It must be safe, and it must be effective. We want the same combination in the organizational structure of our congregations.

When a congregation has a bureaucratic structure, either by design or default, it assigns responsibility to its pastor but divorces that responsibility from the authority needed to fulfill it. So the formula is responsibility *minus* authority, and the result is an organization that may appear safe but is certainly ineffective. Using the pharmaceutical metaphor, we might call the bureaucratic structure a *placebo*. The pastor of this congregation functions merely as an employee.

When a congregation has an authoritarian structure, the fear of which drives most congregations to bureaucracy, it acknowledges the responsibility of the pastor and marries that responsibility to the authority needed to fulfill it—so far, so good. But what if that authority is abused?

Mussolini[1] made the trains run on time (according to his own propaganda), but you might not have liked where some of them would have taken you. The formula here is responsibility plus authority, and the result is an organization that may be effective but is not necessarily safe. A therapeutic metaphor suited to an authoritarian structure might be a narcotic; it works—but watch out! The pastor in this congregation may be seen by many as a dictator.

The bureaucratic arrangement, into which all organizations descend over time unless they are reinvented, is a poor antidote for dictatorship. And the authoritarian arrangement is an unstable solution for the impotence of church bureaucracy. There is a better way: Marry responsibility and authority, as in the authoritarian arrangement, but add the third ingredient of accountability. This formula results in a structure that is both safe and effective—like a lifesaving medicine. The pastor in an accountable structure is set up to be the leader of the flock, a true shepherd in the biblical sense.

When Goals Are Reached

The effect of adding accountability to responsibility and authority is to assure a connection between achievement and reward. As in a sports event, when the goal is reached, the points go up on the board.

To give an account is to give a report. To be held accountable is to experience a consequence linked to the nature of that report. Therefore, accountability in a healthy congregation has two essential components: 1) Periodic reports as to whether responsibility has been fulfilled and whether authority has been abused. 2) Rewards or consequences based on the report, assuming the evidence supports it. What happens if one of these components is missing? Whatever happens, it is something other than accountability.

For example, what if there is little or no reporting? Nothing is more common in ministry organizations than statements of good intentions that nobody checks for results. From musty mimeographs to glossy brochures and eye-popping computer graphics, congregations, denominations, and parachurch organizations try to convince their constituents that faithfulness to say the right things is just as good as fruitfulness to get them done. Someone might object, "*Of course* we have reports—lots of them. We have job descriptions, annual reports, annual reviews—you name it." But the problem with many of these documents is that they recount good activities, good intentions, and good feelings but do not address the only two questions pertinent to genuine accountability: 1) Were the intended ends achieved? and 2) Did the means employed to achieve the ends fall within our guidelines?

On the other hand, what if there is a pertinent report with adequate evidence, but there is no connection to reward or correction? In that case, we have an account but not accountability. It is possible that year after year a pastor might give a clear and credible account of status quo without significant growth and year after year get a raise because a) the pastor loves Jesus and b) Jesus's people love the pastor. Or, the disconnect can happen in reverse: A church might be growing and have an increasingly positive impact on the community, but the highly productive staff is lucky to wrangle a cost-of-living increase, let alone merit pay.

Bottom line: If you don't check on intended results regularly and don't connect what happens next to the nature of those results, you don't have accountability. And if you don't have accountability of pastor to the board, you are fostering either a bureaucracy or a dictatorship, neither of which will help your congregation win in the long run.

Statistics vs. Wins

The goal *of* a football game is to win by scoring the most points. The goals *during* a football game are the means to that win. By analogy, when we speak of goal-setting in ministry, there are two kinds of goals: goals that measure means, and goals that measure ends. Let's call the first kind of goal a *stat* (short for *statistic*) and the second kind of goal a *win*.

Stats are good, but wins are better. Each has its place, but the difference is significant. Stats reflect the quality of the plays and the players, which are means. Wins, however, reflect the achievement of ends. John Carver emphasizes the distinction between ends and means as follows: "Ends describe the difference you seek to make in the lives of clients, patients, students, members, consumers, or community. Accountability for ends has intrinsic importance; accountability for the activities intended to achieve ends is an unnecessary and distracting construct. Your organization does not exist for anything your staff is doing, no matter how well-intended, impressive, politically correct, or even righteous. It exists to make a difference."[1]

TABLE 6.2 Contrasting Statements about Stats & Wins

STATS ...	WINS ...
... quantify the plays.	... quantify the game.
... are marked by points.	... are marked by trophies.
... inform management.	... inform governance.
... measure means.	... measure ends.
... are tactical.	... are strategic.
... are helpful.	... are essential.
... count activities.	... count outcomes.
... are what you sow.	... are what you reap.

Table 6.2 displays contrasting statements pertaining to goals that are set to measure means (stats) and goals that are set to measure ends (wins).

Interpretation and Application

If the board of a congregation is going to hold its lead pastor accountable in a fair and meaningful way, it must agree with the pastor in advance on a set of standards for evaluation. In the Accountable Leadership strategy, this set of standards is recorded in a document called the *Guiding Principles*. The very practice of using written standards of any kind adds the task of interpreting this document prior to the task of applying it. Therefore, we need to lay out a process for the Guiding Principles that covers how the standards are composed, interpreted, applied, and finally used to evaluate what happened.

FIGURE 6.1 Cycle of Accountability

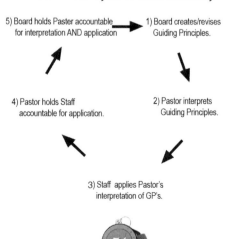

5) Board holds Pastor accountable for interpretation AND application

1) Board creates/revises Guiding Principles.

4) Pastor holds Staff accountable for application.

2) Pastor interprets Guiding Principles.

3) Staff applies Pastor's interpretation of GP's.

Figure 6.1 depicts such a cycle of accountability. First, the board creates or revises the Guiding Principles, by which the performance of the organization will be evaluated. (We'll cover the criteria for creating a good set of Guiding Principles in chapter 12.) Second, the lead pastor—who alone is accountable to the board for the performance of the organization—interprets the Guiding Principles to the staff in the course of directing their work. Third, the staff applies the pastor's interpretation of the Guiding Principles in the course of managing all the ministries of the congregation. Fourth, the lead pastor holds the staff accountable for applying the Guiding Principles. Fifth, the board holds the lead pastor accountable for both interpretation and application of the Guiding Principles. The results of that process influence how the board may revise or create Guiding Principles for the next year.

Who gets to decide what will go into the Guiding Principles? The board does—not the staff, not the congregation, and not the lead pastor (except as a board member). And who gets to interpret the Guiding Principles? The lead pastor does. How wide is the pastor's latitude? The pastor may use any *reasonable* interpretation of the document. Who gets to decide whether or not the interpretation was reasonable? The board does, using the "reasonable person" test: Could a reasonable person have understood what we wrote in the way that the lead pastor has evidently understood it? If the answer is yes, the board has no legitimate complaint with regard to interpretation, though it certainly may revise the Guiding Principles to be more explicit for the future. If the answer is no, the pastor has created a problem and must be subject to correction. Do not misunderstand the application of reasonableness here. The board does not evaluate whether the actions of the pastor and staff are reasonable per se. It simply applies the *reasonable person test* when the pastor's compliance with the Guiding Principles is in question.

Let's analyze the cycle further, using Figure 6.2. Here we distinguish the functions provided by players: board, lead pastor, and staff. The board is there to govern, which happens at Step 1 and Step 5. The pastor is there to lead, which happens at Step 2 and Step 4. The staff is there to manage, which happens at Step 3. Accountability works only when we keep these functions separated and properly related to each other.

Win, Lose, or Draw

When a congregation lacks genuine accountability—as many do—the pastor and staff are retained and perhaps rewarded in their roles as long as they are doing what they are supposed to be doing. That may sound

FIGURE 6.2 Players and Functions on the Cycle of Accountability

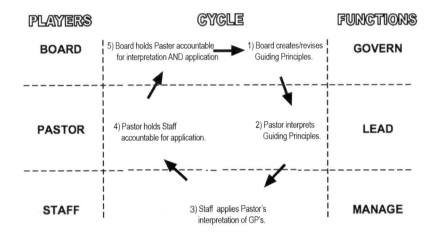

PLAYERS	CYCLE	FUNCTIONS
BOARD	5) Board holds Paster accountable for interpretation AND application → 1) Board creates/revises Guiding Principles.	GOVERN
PASTOR	4) Pastor holds Staff accountable for application. / 2) Pastor interprets Guiding Principles.	LEAD
STAFF	3) Staff applies Pastor's interpretation of GP's.	MANAGE

like accountability, but it is not. When a congregation practices genuine accountability, the pastor and staff are retained and rewarded when they are producing what they are supposed to be producing. Job descriptions with duties to fulfill characterize the first scenario. Annual goals with purposes to fulfill characterize the second.

Accountable pastors lead their team into the fray knowing that every so often they will win, lose, or draw. In the normal course of events, this day of reckoning comes in the form of an annual review of performance and compensation. On occasion, it arrives less predictably in the form of a leadership crisis. In either event, the only two legitimate questions of accountability are: 1) Is the mission being accomplished as we agreed? and 2) Are any agreed upon boundaries being violated in the process? If the answers are yes and no respectively, and dissatisfaction with the pastor remains, the critics are likely pursuing a personal agenda rather than the best interests of the church. Answering the two questions requires the leader to give an account. Holding a leader accountable requires that the leader receive an appropriate response to that account.

What is an appropriate response for pastors winning big on the mission question? Short answer in a free system: a big raise. What about pastors who are losing big on mission? No raise and a year or less to turn around their performance to a reasonable degree. What if there is a "draw" on mission—no great gains or losses? No raise until the congregation starts winning and perhaps two or three years to make that happen. In denominations with predetermined pay scales, reinforcing good performance requires more creativity, e.g. better assignments, resourcing, or flex time in lieu of a salary differential.

What kind of response should a pastor receive for respecting the established boundaries for acceptable behavior? For this accountability question, positive reinforcement should primarily come in the form of public displays of respect and vigorous defense against critics rather than in the form of pay raises. Why no money for this? Because playing within the rules should be a prerequisite for retaining a position. Long ago when my son was thirteen, I was happy to pay him for getting the lawn mowed, but I would never have paid him to refrain from stealing lawn mowers. Negative consequences for violating important boundaries should be swift and certain to make sure that corrections are made—or else. Applying the principle of reasonable interpretation is important so that violations can be judged rightly in the cycle of accountability. And, of course, grace—not to be confused with a lack of truth—should also be applied. Nevertheless, healthy boundaries are there to be respected.

Naturally, there will be occasions when a staff person has a grievance with the lead pastor. A procedure of appeal should be built into the Guiding Principles for those occasions. The procedure should not allow the board to substitute its judgment for supervisory decisions of the lead pastor, but it should ensure that the lead pastor has treated staff in accordance with the Guiding Principles. The bylaws might do well to include a grievance procedure for the lead pastor's benefit as well.

Except in dysfunctional systems, winning is rewarded, losing is penalized, and mediocrity is challenged. Beyond the system itself, there are always natural and spiritual consequences in addition to official accountabilities. From day-to-day church attendees who vote with their feet and their dollars, to the Day when Christ will test with fire the quality of our work in the church (promised in 1 Cor. 3:10–15), there is no doubt that God applies his own accountability to each leader. If a congregation turns its back on the cleansing fire of accountability, it will just have to sit on its blisters.

SUMMARY & PREVIEW

- *A safe and effective organization combines responsibility, authority, and accountability to set up its leader for success.*
- *When a goal is reached, the points go up on the board.*
- *Statistics are good, but wins are better.*
- *The cycle of accountability includes interpretation and application of standards.*
- *Every so often you win, lose, or draw; winning is rewarded, losing is penalized, and mediocrity is challenged—except in dysfunctional systems.*

Part 3 comes next. There we will explore the positions of governance, leadership, management, and ministry of the four major players in the strategy: Congregation, Pastor, Board, and Staff. First up is an overview chapter entitled, "Ministry is a Team Sport."

Note

1. John Carver, *John Carver on Board Leadership: Selected Writings from the Creator of the World's Most Provocative and Systematic Governance Model,* (San Francisco: Jossey-Bass, 2002), 254.

PART THREE

DO WE KNOW WHAT POSITION TO PLAY?

CHAPTER SEVEN

Ministry is a Team Sport

We've heard that a million monkeys at a million keyboards
could produce the complete works of Shakespeare;
now, thanks to the Internet, we know that is not true.
Robert Wilensky

UNITY IS MORE THAN A WARM FUZZY FEELING. It's a source of power for effective mission to the world. Does this mean that Christian leaders and their supporters are going to agree on all points of doctrine and all points of ministry? Yes. In heaven, I suppose. But right now, we need a unity that is both deeper and more available than uniformity of opinion. In Romans 15:5–6 Paul prays, "May the God who gives endurance and encouragement give you the same attitude of mind toward each other that Christ Jesus had, so that with one mind and one voice you may glorify the God and Father of our Lord Jesus Christ" (TNIV). In context, following Christ Jesus means enduring insults similar to what Jesus endured as he carried out his mission of redemption.[1] We need unity of purpose. In *Winning on Purpose* terms, we need to agree together on the Object of the Game.

There is an important place for diversity on the team as well as for unity. But one place you *cannot* have diversity is on the question of mission. If you create a tossed salad of leaders with different agendas, your congregation will suffer one of two fates. Either there will be hard and painful division, or there will be soft and putrid compromise. Amos was not making a riddle when he asked, "Do two walk together unless they have agreed to do so?" (Amos 3:3, TNIV) He was emphasizing a principle.

Wayne Cordeiro has led New Hope Christian Fellowship in Honolulu to grow beyond 11,000 without owning property and to plant over 80 daughter churches around the world. He understands this principle: "Alignment can help build an unstoppable movement able to overcome every obstacle, move every mountain and bridge every impasse. When everyone is in alignment, every daily activity contributes in a more meaningful way to the overall vision of the church."[2]

If the board believes that the purpose of the congregation is primarily to take care of existing members and the staff believes that the purpose of the congregation is primarily to make new disciples and secondarily to take care of existing members, there is going to be a problem. It won't be small, and it won't be pretty. So it is vital to the success of a missional congregation that all the key players share one heart and mind concerning the purpose of the church. If you want an outward-focused ministry, you don't call a pastor whose agenda is to create a fortress for the defense of a theological system, you don't select board members who want to play devil's advocate (the devil has enough advocates already), you don't hire staff who can't manage their ministry for outreach, and you don't receive members who won't agree to support the purpose of the church. At the point of mission, if there is not unity on the team, there will be disaster.

Diversity on the Team

Once we have unity of purpose, i.e. agreement on the mission, what kind of diversity do we need? Let's put it this way: Diversity of agenda is deadly, diversity of background is helpful, and diversity of role is essential.

People from various walks of life can shed light on an issue through different windows, whether ethnic, socio-economic, or professional. With more light, a team can make brighter decisions. As helpful as this *personal diversity* might be, however, there is another type that is absolutely essential for the Accountable Leadership strategy: *functional diversity.*

The board is not the pastor is not the staff is not the congregation. Each of these four players has a distinct and critical contribution to make. If any one of the players fails to make its unique contribution, the team will lose. Later we'll get into the details of each player's responsibility, but the focus for our present discussion is the importance of this kind of diversity for the strength of the team.

Take baseball for example. Different players who have different skills play the positions of pitcher, catcher, infield, and outfield. In the 1930's, Bud Abbott and Lou Costello popularized a comedy sketch known around the world as "Who's on First." Here's a short excerpt:

> You know the fellows' names? *Certainly!*
> Well then who's on first? *Yes!*
> I mean the fellow's name! *Who!*
> The guy on first! *Who!*
> The first baseman! *Who!*
> The guy playing first! *Who is on first!*
> Now whaddya askin' me for? *I'm telling you: Who is on first.*

Well, I'm asking YOU who's on first! *That's the man's name.*
That's who's name? *Yes.*
Well go ahead and tell me. *Who.*
The guy on first. *Who!*
The first baseman. *Who is on first!*
Have you got a contract with the first baseman? *Absolutely.*
Who signs the contract? *Well, naturally!*
When you pay off the first baseman every month, who gets the money?
   Every dollar. Why not? The man's entitled to it.
Who is? *Yes. Sometimes his wife comes down and collects it.*
Who's wife? *Yes.*
All I'm tryin' to find out is what's the guy's name on first base.
   Oh, no—wait a minute, don't switch 'em around. What is on second base.
I'm not askin' you who's on second. *Who is on first.*
I don't know. *He's on third—we're not talkin' 'bout him."[3]*

Reality check: If you are this confused about who is playing what position in the leadership of your congregation, do not expect to hear applause. You will indeed appear ridiculous, but without the audience appreciation.

When parents act like children, we have a dysfunctional family. And when shepherds act like sheep, we have a dysfunctional church. There is no way to have accountable leadership if you do not know who to hold accountable and for what. The *congregation* is there to *minister*. The *pastor* is there to *lead*. The *board* is there to *govern*. The *staff* is there to *manage*. Don't mix up the positions if you are playing to win.[4]

Captain of the Team

Readers of ministry literature have seen many trends come and go. Labels are in for a while; then they are out. *Committee*, for example, has been a bad word since the Church Renewal movement of the 1970's. *Small group, team,* or more recently, *community* is what we want to be. Far more important than the label itself is what we mean by it. This book emphasizes the metaphor of a *team.* But what exactly does "team" mean for the missional congregation? For starters, a team is a community of servants who share the same mission and vision (unity) and are responsible for different roles (diversity) in fulfilling it. And one of those roles is the position of leadership. The team needs a captain.

You might recall that one of the assumptions stated in the Introduction of *Winning on Purpose* is the following: Groups cannot realistically be expected to lead or to be held accountable, but individuals can and should. The individual who is accountable for the overall effectiveness of the congregation is its leader, the pastor.

We are all on the same team, but we need someone to lead. We are all equal in the sight of God, but we need someone to lead. We are all imperfect disciples growing together in Christ, but we still need someone to lead. Groups by their nature don't lead; they are always led. If you come across a group that says, "We work as a team. We don't have a leader," the person saying it the loudest is the leader—or perhaps the leader's puppet. The problem for a group with an unidentified leader is that it has no way to hold this leader accountable for his or her influence. It's better to agree on a designated leader so that expectations are set appropriately according to the purpose of the group.

Larry Osborne, who pastors the innovative North Coast Church near San Diego, uses this analogy for the type of captain a team needs: "I compare the leader to a point guard on a basketball team. Directing the offense falls on his shoulders. That doesn't mean the off guard, forwards, or center can't initiate a play or fast break, but most of the time they'll look to him to take the lead. In a church, a leader sets the agenda, general tone, and direction for ministry. When a tough problem or exciting opportunity comes along, everyone knows to whom to look for direction."[5] In order to win, the team needs a captain who can lead it to victory.

Training and Coaching for the Team

There are pastors and boards that avoid consultation and training. Some may not be aware of the wealth of resources available to them. Some may not want to expose their performance to evaluation. Perhaps others think that training and coaching are only for leaders who are not quite up to the task. Whatever the reason for not getting help, functioning in isolation is not the way of the winning team.

Let's take the lack of awareness problem first. Chances are that the kinds of leaders who would read this book are the kinds of leaders who know about similar resources. Be that as it may, here are a dozen recommended sources for help with congregational ministry:

Accountable Leadership (Kaiser)	www.accountableleadership.org
ChurchSmart Resources (NCD)	www.churchsmart.com
CoachNet (Logan)	www.coachnet.org
Easum, Bandy & Associates	www.easumbandy.com
GHC Network (Church Multiplication)	www.ghcnetwork.org
Gospel Communications	www.gospelcom.net

Griffith Coaching Network	www.*griffithcoaching.com*
Leadership Network	www.*leadnet.org*
NexStep Coaching (Hoyt)	www.*nexstepcoaching.org*
PastorPreneur (Jackson)	www.*pastorpreneur.com*
Purpose-Driven Church (Warren)	www.*pastors.com*
Willow Creek Association (Hybels)	www.*willowcreek.com*

Enough said about lack of awareness. Rise, Peter, click and eat.[6]

Now on to fear of evaluation. There is a lot of this going around. Let's start with one simple reality: Pastors who are leading their congregations to grow are in the minority, at least in the United States and similar Western societies. So if a congregation is growing, especially through new believers, it arguably has (or has had) one of the best pastors in the country. It follows that any evaluation should come as an encouragement and as a way to make a good thing better.

For congregations that are not growing, there are two choices: 1) The congregation can redefine the vision to match the performance. This is like the child who shot arrows at the wooden fence then drew a bulls-eye around each one where it landed. Sadly, this dumbing-down response to doldrums and decline is widespread. Empty churches rent their facilities to other groups and call them "ministry partnerships." Pastors count new activities instead of new disciples. But there is a better alternative. 2) The congregation can begin the journey, in truth and love, toward accountable leadership. And a clear understanding of accountable leadership is half the journey. The other half is implementing an honest yet grace-based plan that sets a pastor up for success, and then waiting to see if success is forthcoming. The grace aspect allows ample time; provides ample support; and, when necessary, offers ample help for transition to another job if the pastor cannot lead the congregation to fulfill its mission. "What?" some might say, "If the pastor can't lead, then we need a new pastor? Isn't that a little harsh?" Not if you treat people with dignity (e.g., generosity with time and money). But each congregation has to make its own decision: Is the purpose of our ministry to provide secure jobs for our staff? Or is the purpose to accomplish our share of the Great Commission?

One reason for resisting consultation remains: the notion that such help is for deficient leaders. But in reality, the opposite is true. Think about the development of athletes. The average player gets average training and coaching. The better player gets better training and coaching. And the exceptional player gets exceptional training and coaching. Why? Because the investment pays off when directed at winners. In 2004 the Boston Red Sox won the World Series for the first time since 1918—by shutting out the legendary New York Yankees. Did the Sox then fire their coaching staff and cancel practices? Hardly. They had that much more to live up to next season.

Wherever your leaders may fall on the spectrum of effectiveness, a team needs training and coaching to improve its game. And as a team sport, ministry is worth the investment.

SUMMARY & PREVIEW

- *The team needs unity on the object of the game.*

- *The team needs a diversity of players and positions.*

- *The team needs a captain who can lead it to victory.*

- *The team needs training and coaching to improve its game.*

Coming next, we begin analyzing the players and positions with a look at the congregation, which plays the position of ministry. The remaining three positions covered in part 3 exist solely to help these ministers succeed.

Notes

1. Cf. Romans 15:3
2. Wayne Cordeiro, *Doing Church as a Team* (Ventura, CA: Regal, 2001), 151.
3. http://www.baseballhalloffame.org/library/research_lists/whos_on_first.htm
4. I stress these distinctions only for grasping and applying the Accountable Leadership strategy. Other respected governance models reflect different approaches. In Bandy's model, for example, the congregation shares in all four functions. In Carver's model, the functions are so separated that the pastor would play no part in determining board policy. In a traditional managing board model, the board would make any decisions it wished and leave the rest to the staff, which it might overrule. Of these alternatives, perhaps only Carver would fully resonate with the zeal for playing to win in Accountable Leadership, but his constrained CEO who merely implements the board's policy is not compatible with a robust, biblical concept of pastoral leadership, in my opinion.
5. Larry W. Osborne, *The Unity Factor: Developing a Healthy Church Leadership Team* (Vista, CA: Owl Concepts, 1989), 52.
6. My apologies to Acts 10:13.

CHAPTER EIGHT

The Congregation Plays Ministry

A winner is someone who recognizes his God-given talents, works his tail off to develop them into skills, and uses these skills to accomplish his goals.
Larry Bird

"THEN CAME A WAR," EXPLAINS JOSEPH, the supervising angel in Frank Capra's classic film, *It's a Wonderful Life*. "Ma Bailey and Mrs. Hatch joined the Red Cross and sewed. Mary had two more babies, but still found time to run the U.S.O. Sam Wainwright made a fortune in plastic hoods for planes. Potter became head of the draft board. Gower and Uncle Billy sold war bonds. Bert, the cop, was wounded in North Africa—got the Silver Star. Ernie, the taxi driver, parachuted into France. Marty helped capture the Remagen Bridge. Harry . . . Harry Bailey topped them all. A Navy flier, he shot down fifteen planes. George? Four-F on account of his ear, George fought the battle of Bedford Falls: Air Raid Warden . . . paper drives . . . scrap drives . . . rubber drives . . . Like everybody else, on V-E Day he wept and prayed. On V-J Day he wept and prayed again."[1]

During the Second World War, nearly everyone in the United States was mobilized in one way or another. Some, like three of my uncles, served in military units. Others, like my father, who designed dredging equipment for military installations, served in civilian support roles. From collecting scrap metal to fighting on the front lines to gathering intelligence to working in factories, men, women, and children served in an enormous variety of capacities. There was a place for every kind of contribution on both the war front and the home front. In the spiritual war over eternal destinies of men and women, there is an even greater cause for mobilization and an even wider range of abilities needed. Christ has distributed gifts to every member of his body, and all of us are called to use them in obedience to his purpose on the front lines and in support of one another behind the lines. Therefore, the position played by the congregation in the Accountable Leadership strategy is *ministry*.

Control vs. Trust

According to Ephesians 4, pastors and other leaders are given by Christ to his Church in order to equip its members to minister. Unfortunately, many congregations are organized for precisely the opposite relationship: members equip the pastor to do the ministry for them. In order to set this relationship right-side up, with leaders leading and ministers ministering, the powerful issue of control vs. trust must be confronted and reversed.

TABLE 8.1 Control Paradigm vs. Trust Paradigm

	CONTROL	TRUST
Pastor	The pastor controls the ministries of the church to see that the people do things a certain way.	The pastor entrusts the minitries of the church to see that the people bear much fruit.
People	The people control the leadership of the church to see that the pastor does things a certain way.	The people entrust the leadership of the church to see that the pastor bears much fruit.
Result	Pastor and people treat each other like children because . . .	Pastors and people treat each other like adults because . . .
Value	. . . doing things a certain way is more important than bearing much fruit.	. . . bearing much fruit is more important than doing things a certain way.
Motto	"If you want something done right, do it yourself."	"This is to my Father's glory that you bear much fruit, showing yourselves to be my disciples.

Because all people (including pastors) share the same human condition, we all like to be in control so that, whenever possible, things are done in the way with which we are most comfortable. So without conscious effort to the contrary, over time congregations tend to fall into the *control paradigm*. Table 8.1 displays the characteristics of a congregation in which an atmosphere of control pervades the organization. Pastors in this paradigm control the ministries of the church. Each area of operation becomes an extension of the pastor's personality and must be carried out according to the pastor's favorite methods. The people in a control paradigm protect their power over the leadership of the church to make sure that the pastor works in a manner that pleases most of the people most of the time, or at least the people of influence. The result is that the pastor and the people treat each other like children because of a deep but unspoken value: Doing things a certain way is more important then bearing much fruit. The motto of the control paradigm is simple: *If you want something done right, do it yourself.* You certainly wouldn't want to trust someone else to do it.

Healthy, growing, and reproducing congregations are characterized more by trust than by control. In the *trust paradigm,* the pastor entrusts the ministries of the church to the people in order to see that the people bear much fruit. The words "to see that" imply accountability for outcomes. In an atmosphere of trust, the people entrust the leadership of the congregation to the pastor in order to see that the pastor bears much fruit as well. Again there is accountability. The result of this paradigm is healthy. The pastor and the people treat each other like adults because they have chosen the opposite value: Bearing much fruit is more important than doing things a certain way. The motto of the trust paradigm comes from John 15:8 "This is to my Father's glory, that you bear much fruit, showing yourselves to be my disciples" (TNIV). Mission results in worship and demonstrates discipleship. These three are not to be separated.

How can we help our congregations move from the fear-based control paradigm to the faith-based trust paradigm? It will never happen by listing the right values on slides or plaques. It will never happen by talking the talk of mission. It will happen only when we place our scalpel on the structures that reinforce doing things a certain way and slice them away so that a new priority on fruitfulness can grow.

Moving the World

In a missional congregation, the members choose to serve newcomers before they serve themselves. The implications of this outward focus include connecting with people who are new to the church, inviting friends who might come to church, and reaching out to those not yet interested in church. There is little point in theological debate over incarnational versus attractional models of evangelism. The same Jesus who said, "Go and make disciples," (Matt. 28:19–20, TNIV) also said "Come, follow me" (Matt. 4:19, TNIV). So let's use both "so that by all possible means [we] might save some." (1 Cor. 9:20, TNIV). Whether we go to them or they come to us, making disciples is our first ministry priority as the body of Christ.

A second essential ministry for the members of the church to provide is congregational care. This ministry is the "one-another" life that is taught throughout the New Testament: Love one another. Serve one another. Bear one another's burdens. Bear with one another. Pray for one another. And so on.

On the one hand, let's not confuse the one-another life of congregational care with the substitute of "pastoral care," such as visitation and counseling by the senior pastor. Naturally the shepherd of the flock cares for the sheep in order to help them grow up, grow wool, and grow more sheep. However, the one-another life of the Christian community is not assigned to the pastor. Rather the pastor is placed in the body to more effectively assign it to the members.

On the other hand, let's not confuse congregational care with a congregation that has an inward focus. The church, like a human body, ought to spend some time on itself for nourishment and rest. These are necessary parts of life, but they are hardly the purpose of life. A strong and missional congregation does a great job of taking care of its own—actually far better than an ingrown congregation does—but it does so as the foundation for reaching a world that needs Jesus Christ.

FIGURE 8.1 Picture of a Strong and Missional Congregation

The Greek mathematician Archimedes celebrated the power of the lever and fulcrum by saying: "Give me a place to stand, and I can move the world." Figure 8.1 depicts a strong and missional congregation that builds strong home-base ministries within the church and leverages them in support of outreach ministries that can move the world.

Home-base ministries are determined by the expectations of the people the congregation is reaching, and so they differ from one culture or subculture to another. For example, in most growing churches across North America, you might find programming for child-care, worship services, facilities, finances, children's programs, student ministries, small groups, and various classes or seminars. These ministries strengthen the base of the congregation.

FIGURE 8.2 Picture of a Strong but Inward Congregation

However, as depicted in Figure 8.2, many congregations give only lip service to the Great Commission to make disciples of all nations; instead they merely gather and serve disciples that have already been made. These folks may be committed to each other, to sound doctrine, and even to mission—in theory or by others in faraway lands. However, with a little imagination you can overhear the pastor and worship leader in this figure discussing their philosophy of ministry: "See, we believe in moving the world," assures the pastor, "Just look at our flag." "Amen," responds the worship leader, "Let's sing and dance around some more!" The home-base becomes an end in itself, proclaiming in effect, "Give us a place to stand and then—well, then we'll have a place to stand!"

The opposite distortion, though found less often, also exists. Figure 8.3 depicts a congregation that is decidedly missional in its focus but precariously weak in its ability to do much about it. Whether intention-ally or not, this group fails to build a strong home-base from which to reach out. The lever analogy for home-base and outreach ministries is not original with me, but the first time I drew this kind of diagram during a consultation was for an inner city congregation outside of Auckland, New Zealand. The pastor was a dedicated servant of God who had gathered a small community of Christians interested in living out their faith in a depressed community. Every scarce resource was used in one outreach program or another. However, little attention had been given to growing and nurturing the individuals and families needed to sustain and expand this missional endeavor. The pastor's dilemma was whether to continue struggling in their urban setting or to relocate in a suburb nearby. I rec-ommended that he develop the new site to strengthen the workers and redevelop the current site to deploy them.

FIGURE 8.3 Picture of a Weak but Missional Congregation

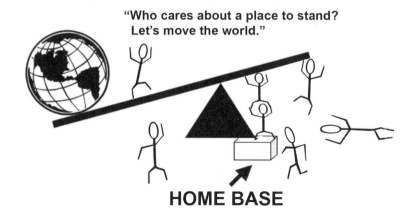

"Who cares about a place to stand?
Let's move the world."

HOME BASE

Accountability—Official and Otherwise

As the congregation plays the position of ministry, it serves others first and itself second. There remains a third responsibility of the congregation: the duty either to affirm and support its leadership or else to find leadership that it can affirm and support. Polity may determine the official account-ability of the pastor and the board to the congregation, but feet and dol-lars determine the real accountability of the organization to its members.

Regardless of polity, members of most congregations have at least three natural ways to hold its officers accountable for success in mission: The first way is to select a winning pastor; even hierarchical denominations generally give congregations a voice on this critical choice. The second way is to instigate a winning attitude, using the power of positive speech; it's a kind of "anti-gossip"—catching people doing something *right* and talking it up. The third way is to reward a winning record; give more generously when and where there is evidence of fruitfulness.

In addition to these natural means of accountability, most congregations formally grant their approval of certain decisions, especially authorizing who will lead them and within what parameters. From a *Winning on Purpose* point of view, *voting in the church matters primarily with reference to the pastor's leadership*. If the members are voting to call a senior pastor, that ballot is critical to the health and growth of a congregation. It will set the ministry up to win or lose for years to come. Members must show up and make sure they get the right leader. If a congregation has an effective pastor and the members are voting on a high stakes issue for the pastor's vision, that ballot also is critical. Don't underestimate the corrosive combination of vocal opponents and silent supporters. Members should show up and stand up for a leader in whom they believe. What about congregational votes that bear little relationship to pastoral leadership? In a healthy environment, such approvals are pared down to a very short list and routinely granted (after a few wisecracks from critics about rubber-stamping). In unhealthy environments, such matters become distractions as unaccountable influencers try to take leadership into their own hands and away from the pastor.

What can members do if the pastor is not leading the congregation to succeed and if the board will do nothing about it? One option I advise against is to stay but to stop giving, or to play games with designated giving. If the situation is that bad, there is a more honorable alternative: simply leave well. This act will be a true service to the cause of Christ, to the congregation, and to family and friends. Leaving well means that a person a) does his or her homework to make sure the leadership is not on a road to winning, b) tells people the truth about why he or she is leaving, and c) finds a growing congregation whose leaders he or she can support. If enough people do this, the leaders may begin to get the message; and, at worst, those who leave are in a place where they can be positive rather than divisive.

The congregation is the ultimate player in the Accountable Leadership strategy. The board, pastor, and staff play their positions only so that the congregation can effectively do the work of the ministry—moving the world for Christ and supporting each other in that mission through the Church!

SUMMARY & PREVIEW

- *Biblically, the leaders equip the members to minister, not vice versa.*

- *In a missional congregation, the members serve outsiders ahead of each other.*

- *A second essential ministry for the members to provide is congregational care.*

- *Polity determines the official accountability of the board to the members, but feet and dollars determine the real accountability of the board to the members.*

Next we'll consider why the leadership position is needed and why the pastor is the one to play it. Three aspects of leadership that must be embraced by the pastor and three distinct modes of leading the board, the staff, and the congregation are identified. We'll end with a caution about what Accountable Leadership can and cannot do for pastors.

Note

1. *It's a Wonderful Life.* Screenplay found at http://geocities.com/classicmoviescripts/script/itsawonderfullife.txt. By way of trivia the names of Bert and Ernie on Sesame Street came from this film.

CHAPTER NINE
The Pastor Plays Leadership

The moral and ethical failure of a pastor will devastate a church,
but a godly pastor who is incompetent is no blessing.
Gary McIntosh

ONE NIGHT IN 1962, RAY CHARLES INSERTED A COUNTRY SONG into his rhythm and blues repertoire at the Saenger Theatre in St. Louis. As depicted in the motion picture *Ray*, that evening a man new to his entourage made a snap decision to order the lights turned down in favor of a spotlight on the piano. This calmed the confused audience and prepared them to give Charles's risky selection of "I Can't Stop Loving You" a hearing. The crowd was moved from questioning whispers to standing ovation. Ray Charles asked the man after the concert who had told him to change the lights. "Nobody," he replied, "It just needed to be done, so I did it." Charles then remarked how much he liked the man's initiative as opposed to the more common attitude: "That's not my job."

A leader sees what needs to happen and finds a way to make it happen. Leith Anderson, who Lyle Schaller describes as America's wisest pastor, goes so far as to define leadership in these terms: "Leadership is figuring out what needs to be done and then doing it."[1]

In the Accountable Leadership strategy, the pastor plays leadership. To explain how this position is played, we will answer four questions about the pastor:

1) Why is one primary leader needed?
2) What kind of character is needed in the pastor as leader?
3) How is pastoral leadership exercised in the contexts of board, staff, and congregation?
4) How far can the Accountable Leadership strategy go toward ensuring effective pastoral leadership?

The Case for a Primary Leader

A primary leader is essential to church-wide accountability. There can and should be many leaders *in* the congregation, but accountability requires that there be one leader *of* the congregation. Groups by nature exhibit properties such as personal alliances, eclectic compromise, and mutual protection. These properties make well-led groups the perfect vehicles for building community and teamwork. However, these same properties make the group a poor substitute for the accountable leader. Governance by a group—good. Ministry by a group—fine. Leadership by a group—I don't think so. Groups don't lead; they are led. It makes no functional difference whether you replace the primary leader with a town hall meeting, a committee, a task force, a board, a team, a ministry community, or a couple of co-pastors; plurality diffuses accountability. That's precisely why relatively few are willing to become leaders; for true leaders, there is no place to hide. Theoretically, you could try to hold a group accountable by firing or dissolving the entire group for poor performance. However, few congregations would do this even once, let alone repeatedly as an ongoing practice. Therefore, in the normal course of church life, if anyone is going to be held accountable for the healthy growth of congregation, then someone must be held accountable for it: that someone is the leader.

A primary leader can best align resources with the mission. Groups without a primary leader tend to be aimless and anxious, rather than courageous and risk-taking. Before Haggai mobilized the leaders and people of Jerusalem to complete the rebuilding of the Temple following the Exile, they were convinced that they did not have the resources and that the time was not right. After the prophet's strong word from God, the people lined up with the mission and resumed work on the Temple in less than four weeks. In response to their obedience, God prospered them and multiplied their resources. While only God truly creates resources, a primary leader creatively discovers, mobilizes, and then aligns resources with the overall mission.

A primary leader is needed to cast a clear and compelling vision. There is a reason that the army bugler is a solo act. Lives are on the line, and the soldiers need a clear, decisive signal for action. A senior pastor can delegate any number of pastoral duties to others on the team, depending on the needs of the ministry as it grows: counseling, administration, even preaching—at least in part. But one core duty that the lead pastor can never give away is the role of chief vision-caster. This premise does not mean that only a natural visionary can be the primary leader, for there are many ways to formulate the vision with the help of others; but it does mean that only the primary leader can adequately champion the vision for the congregation as a whole.

Successful mission communities in the Bible had a primary leader. From the people of God as a family under Abraham, Jacob, and Joseph to the people of God as a nation under Moses, Joshua, Gideon, Deborah, Samuel, David, and Nehemiah, the Old Testament contains nothing to commend the absence of a primary leader. To the contrary, the assumption is: "Strike the shepherd, and the sheep will be scattered."[2] Nevertheless, some may be quick to write off 39 of the 66 books in the Bible as irrelevant to leadership in the New Testament Church. Do we not find not multiple apostles, multiple elders, and multiple deacons in the congregations and ministries described in Acts through Revelation? Indeed we do, but when we first read of the apostles in Acts 1, we see that Peter is leading them. When we read of the mission bands beginning in Acts 13, we see that either Barnabas or Paul is leading them. When we read of the Jerusalem Council in Acts 15, we see that James is leading it. When we read of the Ephesian elders in the Pastoral Epistles (cf Acts 20), we see that Timothy was appointing and overseeing them. When we read of the seven congregations of Revelation 1–2, we see each one is represented by a single messenger—whether earthly or celestial—and not by a group.

Gene Getz, a leading light of the Church Renewal movement dating from the 1970s, originally advocated a plurality of elders acting in unanimity as the true biblical form of church leadership. If there was a full-time pastor he was "only one among several qualified men designated as spiritual leaders in the congregation."[3] Through his decades of experience as a church planter, large church pastor, seminary professor, and author, it is instructive to see how dramatically his emphasis has changed. In the second edition of *Sharpening the Focus of the Church,* Getz revised the section on church leadership to make room for a primary leader.[4] In his recent volume, *Elders and Leaders,* Getz devotes an entire chapter to making an exegetical case for the following assertion: "The New Testament definitely teaches and illustrates that when there is a plurality of leadership, someone needs to function as the primary leader of the team."[5] It is not the purpose of this volume to debate the competing claims of various church polities to a biblical foundation. Instead, *Winning on Purpose* simply suggests here that the fluid and missional leadership structures in the New Testament era included a place for each group to have a primary leader.

Successful mission communities in historical and contemporary experience have a primary leader. Where would the Celtic church have been without the leadership of Patrick? Where would the Reformation have been without Luther or Calvin? Where would the Great Awakenings have been without

Wesley, Whitfield, or Finney? Where would the modern missionary movement have been without Carey, Judson, Taylor, or Moody? High impact leaders of the twentieth century are still so recent as to evoke both gratitude and criticism. Whatever the judgment of history may become, the last hundred years would not have been the same without Billy Sunday, Aimee Semple McPherson, Billy Graham, Martin Luther King Jr., Mother Teresa, Rick Warren, and David Yonggi Cho. The list for our new century will likely be dominated by African, Asian, and Hispanic names where the Church is most rapidly growing. For each of these notable movement leaders through the ages, there are thousands of local congregations and ministry organizations led by a pastor or director with a name unsung by most but well-known to One. Ironically, even in movements that champion team and community in contrast to primary leaders, you will find primary leaders who create and orchestrate these movements.

Character of the Pastor as Leader

If the congregation needs a pastor to serve as its primary leader, what kind of person is equal to the task? In both the Old and New Testaments, people who were trusted with positions of responsibility were expected to exhibit godliness in their personal and interpersonal behavior. Acting as an ancient organizational consultant, Jethro recommended to his son-in-law Moses that he choose people who had integrity and feared God (see Exodus 18:21). Over a millennium later, the apostles used a similar standard for those who would distribute food to the widows in the early Jerusalem church. Those who were chosen for this responsibility had to be filled with the Holy Spirit, and they had to be wise (see Acts 6:3). 1 Timothy 3 and Titus 1 offer detailed lists of character qualities for men and women appear as prerequisites for responsible positions in the congregation. These passages give expectations for personal reputation as well as an expectation of strength, reflected by terms like *capable, wisdom, able to, know how, and manage well*. Therefore, something beyond good behavior and reputation is required in the character of those who lead. Let's consider the integrity of a lead pastor with reference to the three elements that comprise the Accountable Leadership strategy: Responsibility (the object of the game), Authority (the rules of the game), and Accountability (the scoring of the game).

TABLE 9.1 Defensive vs. Responsible Statements

What Defensive "Leaders" Say	What Responsible Leaders Say
That's not my job, so I'm not going to do it.	That needs to be done, so I'll see that it is.
The people here just don't want to change.	I need a plan to overcome resistance.
This area is too unchurched for me to grow this congregation or start new ones.	This area is ripe for reaching unchurched people if I can learn to connect with them.
This area is too churched for me to grow this congregation or start new ones	This area is ripe for reaching dechurched people if I can learn to connect with them.
You can't grow a large church in this area because there aren't any of them here.	I have a great opportunity here to develope a high profile ministry if I design it right.
You can't grow a large church in this area because there is one or more here already.	I will learn from large churches here while reaching people that they do not.
I'm so new here that I better tread lightly.	I'm so new here that I better start strong.
If I try to lead change here, I could lose my job and be forced to go someplace else.	As I try to lead change here, I trust God to take care of me—here or someplace else.
The dysfunctional systems in this congregation don't let me lead people forward in mission.	I need to change or work around dysfunctional systems to lead people forward in mission.
Only God can change this church; all I can do is pray and accept whatever happens.	Only God can change this church; I will pray and lead boldly in faith that he will.

Table 9.1 offers a list of comparative statements representing the difference between a mere officeholder on the defense and a leader who embraces responsibility. Responsibility refers to the scope of work to be accomplished, not in terms of activities but in terms of results. When applied to congregational ministry, responsibility requires that the pastor and the board agree together on what the mission of the church is and on who is charged with leading the church to fulfill that mission. So the character of an effective lead pastor includes the commitment to *take responsibility*. Taking responsibility does not mean accepting blame for everything or trying to control everything. It means controlling what can be controlled,

influencing other things, and working with or around the rest. The responsible pastor places mission above self-interest: "Depending on the grace and Spirit of God, it's up to me to lead this congregation to succeed in its mission or else step aside for someone who can."

From responsibility we move to the way a lead pastor uses authority. Whereas responsibility relates to the outcomes to be achieved, authority relates to the means needed to achieve them. What kind of person can we trust with authority? Let's shape our answer by identifying two types we *cannot* trust with authority: 1) someone who will abuse legitimate authority, and 2) someone who will fail to utilize legitimate authority. Both become dangerous when placed into leadership roles. Jesus warned his disciples of leaders who abused their authority to serve themselves instead of others: "You know that those who are regarded as rulers of the Gentiles lord it over them, and their high officials exercise authority over them. Not so with you. Instead, whoever wants to become great among you must be your servant, and whoever wants to be first must be slave of all. For even the Son of Man did not come to be served, but to serve, and to give his life as a ransom for many."[6] Authority is abused when it is diverted from its mission to the benefit of the leader or when the leader fails to respect the boundaries that create legitimate authority. On the other hand, the weak leader who fails to utilize authority is just as dangerous. We count on a judge to make the ruling. We count on a pilot to fly the plane. We count on a shepherd to lead the flock; and when this doesn't happen, the flock is placed at risk. Peter wrote to fellow leaders in the church: "Be shepherds of God's flock that is under your care, watching over them—not because you must, but because you are willing, as God wants you to be; not pursuing dishonest gain, but eager to serve; not lording it over those entrusted to you, but being examples to the flock. And when the Chief Shepherd appears, you will receive the crown of glory that will never fade away."[7] This passage says it all: Don't shirk your authority, don't abuse your authority, and don't forget that Christ wields the final authority. Jesus is the ultimate and only model that we need in order to see what a servant-leader looks like. Jesus was a leader who served and a servant who led. He was neither a tyrant-leader nor a servant-wimp. Pastors can destroy congregations with arrogance or with cowardice, so we need pastors who exhibit both humility and strength.

We have addressed the character of the responsible pastor and the authoritative pastor. But what about the traits of an accountable pastor? What we are seeking is a leader who is committed to give an account of whether the responsibility has been fulfilled and the boundaries have been respected, and to be held accountable for that result and compliance through the application of positive or negative consequences. Only a person of integrity and character is willing to submit to real accountability. Think about what this really means for lead pastors. It means that they must be willing to have pay raises based not on how much people like them but on how much they are actually accomplishing. It means that if the rules they have agreed to are broken, they will be confronted and required to make changes in the way they do things or in the way that people under their leadership do things. It means that if all their best efforts and prayers cannot lead their congregation to grow and multiply, they will leave their position so that the congregation can find a more effective leader for its needs and so that they can find a more suitable ministry for their capabilities. In *Hit the Bullseye* Paul Borden describes the lack of accountability that characterized the American Baptist Churches of the West prior to a radical change of course in 1997, which ended the routine rotation of non-growth pastors. Deep in the culture was an expectation that "if a pastor was perceived as a 'loyal soldier' that pastor would always be helped by the region to find a new pastorate" regardless of track record. Leaving a congregation healthy and growing was not essential. Leaving a congregation dysfunctional and dying was not disqualifying. Curing this ailment required shock therapy: "Therefore…we communicated that the region would no longer help any pastor find another pastorate in the region if the congregation they were leaving was not growing. We would offer them some help to find a congregation to pastor in one of the other thirty-three American Baptist regions, but not this one. As almost anyone can imagine, this announcement was met with shock and disbelief. It was said that this was no way for a region to act and that it was a violation of one of its very purposes for existing. There was even more anger when pastors actually found out that we meant it . . . "[8]

From *why* the congregation needs a lead pastor and *what kind* of person that must be, we turn to the question of *how:* How does the pastor lead in the three different arenas of board, staff, and congregation?

Modes of Leading for Three Arenas

In the context of the board, the pastor leads primarily by inspiring. It is essential that as the spiritual leader of the congregation, the senior pastor be not only a full voting member of the board but a key officer on the board as well. Granted, the pastor should not normally be the chairperson because accountability is enhanced by designating a separate person to keep the board on task. Rather, the pastor's special position on the board might be called that of a CVO: Chief Vision Officer. As the board deliberates on crafting or revising the

Guiding Principles, which articulate the mission of the congregation and boundaries for acceptable behavior in pursuit of that mission, the pastor is the primary member to set the tone, guide the discussion, lead the praying, apply the Scriptures, and inspire confidence in the mission.

In the context of the staff, the pastor leads primarily by directing. For the success of the mission, the unity of the congregation, and the best interests of all the individuals involved, the staff works for the lead pastor. That includes hiring and firing, promoting and demoting, raising and cutting, assigning and reassigning. The congregation has approved the lead pastor and other board members. The lead pastor and other board members have agreed upon boundaries for acceptable dealings with staff. But within those boundaries, every decision about the staff is the lead pastor's call to make. This clear and single line of accountability is essential. To the degree that the board or congregation interfere with that line, mission is derailed, unity is fractured, and individuals are injured.

For fifteen years I served as the senior pastor of congregations that I founded. However, in the year 2000 I went to work on the denominational staff of the American Baptist Churches of the West. The executive minister became my boss. He hired me, and he could fire me. Did this distress me? Quite the opposite: I realized that if my results satisfied his goals and my methods did not violate his standards, my position would be secure and rewarding. If I couldn't produce wins or play within the rules, I would need to take some corrective action or, if I failed within an ample period of time, find another job. What if the board or even the churches of the ABCW had to approve my employment or compensation? The static of politics would distort my accountability. Ever lurking in the background would be the reality that satisfying my boss was good but maybe keeping most of the board or church delegates happy was more important—even if that made my boss unhappy.

Multiple lines of accountability lead only to confusion, division, and pain. Don't inflict this fate on the ministry or the people that you love.

In the context of the congregation, the pastor leads primarily by teaching. No pastoral task is more sacred or beneficial than bringing the Word of God to bear on the minds, hearts, and hands of God's people. Integral to the Great Commission is teaching the growing number of new disciples to obey everything commanded by Christ. *Teaching to obey* means that this mode of leadership does not culminate in knowledge but in behavior. Talking formally, as in preaching, and informally, as in conversation, is part of teaching but no more so than personal example. If pastors don't employ their gifts to serve the mission, don't tithe their income to fund the mission, and don't schedule their time to accomplish the mission, they should not be surprised if calls to commitment from their pulpits go no further than the notebooks of their people.

The pastor must be the great communicator to the congregation. That does not require great oratory, but it does require a clear and compelling message about the love, truth, and purposes of God. This message must also be fitted to the specific needs of the individual congregation and the community it seeks to reach. Teaching as a mode of leadership is not the disinterested transmission of information; it is inspiration and persuasion aimed to mobilize God's people for mission.

Limitations of Accountable Leadership

Since the pastor leads the local church in the three arenas of board, staff, and congregation, it is an understatement to say that the Accountable Leadership strategy requires the pastor to be an effective leader. However, it is important to understand what accountability can and cannot do to ensure that a congregation actually has an effective leader in the pastor's position. Table 9.2 lays out some of the differences.

TABLE 9.2 What to Expect from Accountability

Accountability Can:	Accountability Cannot:
Set up a congregation for success	Guarantee success to a congregation
Defend a pastor during unfair attacks	Keep a pastor from unfair attacks
Make a competent pastor better	Make an incompetent pastor good
Attract and keep an effective pastor	Provide a pastor with permanent job security
Ensure that a pastor's successes are rewarded	Get a pastor a raise in the absence of success
Make removing a pastor fair and rare	Make removing a pastor easy or painless
Give a pastor the best chance to succeed	Ensure that a given pastor will succeed
Correct unacceptable behavior	Prevent unacceptable behavior
Keep the congregation fruitful	Keep every member happy
Encourage people to do their best work	Substitute for asking God to give the increase

Winning on Purpose devotes so much attention to explicating an organizational model that it is important to repeat at this point that structural models are neither the purpose of the congregation nor the most critical variable in fulfilling that purpose. The purpose is mission, and the critical variable is pastoral leadership. What *Winning on Purpose* can do for a congregation is to provide a system to help identify, attract, retain, and support a strong senior pastor. However, both leading that system and following it are dependent on the character and competency of the people in the system. If a congregation has a pastor who is not able lead it to grow—even with the freedom and support of the Accountable Leadership strategy over a reasonable period of time—and neither the congregation nor the pastor is willing to make room for a new leader, then no organizational system will help. The problem is one of courage and integrity rather than strategies and tactics.

Whether backstage at a Ray Charles concert or up front in a local congregation, it is absolutely clear that someone needs to take responsibility for what needs to be done. In the local church, that someone is the senior pastor.

SUMMARY & PREVIEW

• *A strong primary leader is essential to the mission of the church.*

• *A pastor with integrity embraces responsibility, authority, and accountability.*

• *The pastor leads differently in three arenas: board, staff, and congregation.*

• *Caution: Accountable Leadership supports leaders but does not create them.*

The next chapter covers the position of governance, played by the board. After distinguishing governance from the positions of leadership, management, and ministry, the chapter goes on to describe a four-part job description for the governing board.

Notes

1. Leith Anderson, Leadership That Works: Hope and Direction for Church and Parachurch Leaders in Today's Complex World, (Minneapolis: Bethany House, 1999), 51. Schaller's description of Anderson appears in his endorsement on the back cover.
2. Zechariah 13:7, TNIV, cf 1 Kings 22:17.
3. Gene Getz, Sharpening the Focus of the Church, (Chicago: Moody Press, 1974), 121.

4. Getz, Sharpening the Focus of the Church: Extensively Revised, (Wheaton: Victor Books, 1984), 177–79.

5. Getz, Elders and Leaders: God's Plan for Leading the Church, (Chicago: Moody Press, 2003), 217. Getz explains his shift in the Introduction, pp. 17–19.

6. Mark 10:42–45 (TNIV)

7. 1 Peter 5:2–4 (TNIV)

8. Paul D. Borden, Hit the Bullseye: How Denominations Can Aim the Congregation at the Mission Field, (Nashville: Abingdon Press, 2003), p. 48.

CHAPTER TEN

The Board
Plays Governance

How can you govern a country which has 246 varieties of cheese?
Charles De Gaulle

"As many of you know, Condi's true ambition is beyond my power to grant," announced President George W. Bush. "She would really like to be the commissioner of the National Football League. I'm glad she's put those plans on hold once again. The nation needs her. I urge the Senate to promptly confirm Condoleezza Rice as America's 66th Secretary of State."[1]

Close advisor to the President, speaker of four languages, author, political scientist, university provost, pianist, and figure skater (though not lately), why would the world's most influential African-American woman want to be a sports commissioner? Maybe it's for love of the game, or maybe it's one of the few things she hasn't already mastered. Whatever the reason, if she ever were to become the commissioner of the NFL, she would switch from playing by the rules to making them.

In the Accountable Leadership strategy, the board plays governance. It's a position that is one part commissioner, one part umpire, one part scorekeeper, and one part cheerleader. In the pages that follow, we will distinguish governance from the other key positions in the *Winning on Purpose* metaphor and explain who the board represents, where the board sets the standards, what the board monitors, and how the board supports the pastor. Finally, we will identify who makes sure that these vital tasks of governance actually get done and get done right.

The Governance Distinctive

There is nothing more critical for using the strategy in this book than the distinction of *governance* in contrast to *leadership, management,* and *ministry.* For our purposes, ministry is the position that provides outreach first, then care for one another; it is played by the members. Management is the position that provides equipping and coordination in each area of ministry; it is played by the staff. Leadership is the position that provides vision, direction, and teaching to achieve the mission; it is played by the pastor. Governance is not synonymous with ministry, management, or leadership. It does not call the plays. It does not execute the plays. So what good is it?

Governance provides the crucial but often missing combination of accountability and support for the pastor, which safely allows the pastor to empower the members for ministry. Furnishing this missing combination is the very heart of the Accountable Leadership strategy.

TABLE 10.1 Telling the Players Apart in Winning on Purpose

POSITIONS	PLAYERS	FUNCTIONS	METAPHORS
Ministry	Members	Outreach first then Care for One Another	Teammates or Champions, Athletes, etc.
Management	Staff	Equipping and Coordination	Assistant Coaches and Specialists
Leadership	Pastor	Vision, Direction, and Teaching	Head Coach or Quarterback, Captain, etc.
Governance	Board	Accountability and Support	Commissioner, Umpire, Scorekeeper, & Cheerleader

Table 10.1 compares the four positions. First comes the position of Ministry, played by the Members. This is where the action takes place. The other positions exist only to support the ministry of the members to do outreach first and congregational care second. This order of priority is based on an outward-focused congregation. The game is won or lost right here, by the members, and nowhere else. The members are the ministers of the congregation or, in *Winning on Purpose* metaphors: the teammates, athletes, or champions. Though the individuals on the board are also members and therefore ministers, the board does not exist to do ministry; it exists to provide accountability and support to the pastor so that the pastor can mobilize the members to do ministry.

Next is the Management position, played by the Staff. Staff includes the paid or volunteer heads of all ministries and operations. Their function is to equip and coordinate ministries done by the members. They work under the direction of the pastor. In terms of the metaphor, they are assistant coaches and specialists covering all the various divisions of the team under the direction of the head coach. The board does not exist to manage the congregation; that's what the staff is for. The board stays two steps removed from managing, i.e. the orchestration of means. It does not interact with the staff directly, but only through the pastor. It is critical to Accountable Leadership that the board be prevented—through vigilance against old habits—from sliding into management.

Finally, on Table 10.1 we come to the last non-governance position, the position of Leadership, played by the Pastor. By *pastor,* I mean the senior or lead pastor responsible for the entire congregation. The function of the pastor is to provide vision, direction, and teaching. The underlying premise is that congregations will succeed or fail in the long term based on effective pastoral leadership more than any other human factor. There may be an exception somewhere, but not in the hundreds of congregations I have worked with or the thousands I have studied. So what does this mean for the contribution of the board with respect to the pastor? It means that the board must govern in a way that holds up the pastor as the leader. The board itself should not lead the congregation because 1) groups are *led* more naturally and with less dysfunction than they *lead*, and 2) there are excellent theological, biblical, and practical arguments for strong pastoral leadership. Aubrey Malphurs has devoted an excellent chapter to the topic in *Planting Growing Churches for the 21st Century.* I recommend that you read it. As an alternative, if you accept my premise that groups don't lead by nature, you can render the question moot and read something else.[2]

Now that we have distinguished governance from the positions of leadership, management, and ministry, we understand what governing boards must not do. The pastor is there to lead, the staff is there to manage, and the members are there to minister. A board that inserts itself into these three functions not only interferes with the other three players; it abandons its own essential work in the process. Now for a four-point job description describing what governing boards do.

Trustees for Whom?

The first task of a governing board is representation. The individuals on the board are appointed in order to safeguard something for someone.

Whether or not the title is used and whether or not the legal status is attached, the people on the board are, in fact, trustees: they have been given a sacred trust. This begs the question: Just who is it that the board represents? Among the valuable contributions of John Carver's governance model is his discussion of nonprofit organizations having "moral owners."[3] In business, unlike the church or other nonprofits, the owners of the enterprise are the shareholders; this form of ownership is a matter of legal record and may be bought or sold. What is the counterpart to the shareholder for the congregation?

Who owns the local church? Most but not all congregations have a membership roll of some kind. Do the members own the church? All congregations by definition are composed of congregants, both members and nonmembers who attend, relate to each other, and talk about "our church." Do the congregants own the church? In a legal sense, the answer is no (though we've seen plenty of people in churches act as if it were their personal property), but what about moral ownership?

For us, the concept of moral ownership must be addressed in theological and missional terms, and not merely in sociological terms. Theologically speaking, who owns the Church? This is not a hard question. The Church belongs to Jesus Christ. He invented it with the words, "On this rock I will build *my* church." The Church is *his* bride, *his* body, *his* temple, *his* people, *his* . . . well, you get the idea.[4] If the whole Church belongs to Jesus Christ, it follows that every local expression of the Church belongs to him as well. So Christ himself is the ultimate Owner of "our" congregation. Anyone who has a problem with that has a bigger problem than any organizational strategy can fix.

Moving from theology to mission: Who on earth is the congregation for? For the outward-focused congregation, the answer is clear: outsiders first and insiders second. For the inward-focused congregation, the answer is also clear and is broadcast, so to speak, every Sunday morning at 11:00 on WIII-FM ("What Is In It—For Me").

Putting the theological and missional dimensions together, we can finally define the moral ownership of our congregation in these words: *Our congregation belongs to Christ and to those who Christ calls his Church to serve.* Jesus's mission was seeking and saving those who are lost. It still is. And we are his presence on earth to carry it out. The first and ultimate allegiance of the board is to Jesus Christ. End of story. Others may vote, give money, or make demands, but these influences must not confuse the board members as to 1) Who has entrusted his precious possession to them in order to break down the gates of hell on earth and 2) To Whom they must ultimately give account for that offensive mission.

Board members are not there to represent personal agendas, people groups, or ministry departments. The Owner of the congregation is the Lord of the Church; he alone chooses the beneficiaries: first the lost sheep, then the gathered flock (Luke 15:1–7). The board represents Jesus and his mission to people in the world, who he died to redeem.[5]

Defining the Guiding Principles

We have just explained the first task of the board: to represent Christ as the owner of the congregation. The second piece of the board's job is writing and adjusting a living set of Guiding Principles designed to ensure that the mission of the Owner is carried out within parameters acceptable to the Owner. These Guiding Principles are an essential piece of equipment for the *Winning on Purpose* congregation, and later we'll go over them in detail. But for now, let's focus on why the task of creating and improving the Guiding Principles is a core responsibility of the board.

A few pages back we said that governance provides the crucial but often missing combination of accountability and support for the pastor. Now it's a fine thing to say that the board will hold the pastor accountable and will support the pastor's leadership, but just how is that supposed to happen and according to what standards? The Guiding Principles document, on which the board and pastor agree and from which they do their work, is the answer to that question. They may revise this agreement at any time, but accountability and support will flow out of whatever the Guiding Principles say during a given period.

The three basic "elements of the game" are delineated by the Guiding Principles: the object of the game (Mission Principles), the rules of the game (Boundary Principles), and how to keep score (Accountability Principles). The Mission Principles are addressed from the board to the pastor; they prescribe for him or her the essential outcomes the congregation exists to achieve. The Boundary Principles are also addressed from the board to the pastor; they prohibit for him or her the kinds of tactics and conditions that are unacceptable en route to fulfilling the Mission Principles. The Accountability Principles are addressed from the board to its chairperson. They define for the chairperson the process of governance agreed upon by the board and the pastor. This third set of principles tells the chairperson how to keep the board on track for three accountabilities: the accountability of the board to the Owner and his beneficiaries, the accountability of the board to itself for the integrity of its work, and the accountability of the pastor to the board for fulfilling the mission and respecting the boundaries.

There is no more central work of the board in the Accountable Leadership strategy than composing and refreshing the Guiding Principles. For the board, the pastor, and the staff to do their work with confidence, these principles must be written. And they must be concise, comprehensive, current, broad, and available.

Keeping Score and Calling Penalties

The board relates to the Owner of the team and defines the rules of the game. These first two tasks are analogous to the work of a commissioner in the sports metaphor. But the board does more. Like a combination umpire and score-keeper, the board monitors the game as it is being played in order to call a penalty when the boundaries are violated and to award points when a goal is achieved. So, ensuring performance is the third essential piece of the board's job description. If this level of accountability sounds heavy, consider the alternatives.

One alternative is a board that takes no kind of action in response to the pastor's performance. The paycheck says, *"You're a nice person, and we're comfortable having you in the position of pastor; here's what we think you need."* It does not say, *"You are leading the congregation more (or less) effectively with regard to the standards we agreed upon; here's what we think you're worth."* Separating compensation from performance might seem to create a pleasant road to travel, but it is not one that leads to a winning pastor or congregation in terms of mission accomplished. Achievers won't stay, and "stay-ers" won't achieve under these conditions.

The other alternative is a board that controls the pastor. The pastor is the "spiritual leader" and can preach with relative freedom, but anything involving money, staff, or programs had better please the right people. The expectations are hidden, but they are out there somewhere, buried shallow along the trail, waiting to blow the legs out from under the unsuspecting pastor who makes a wrong move in the minefield.

After faithfully serving a congregation for seven years, Pastor Ted Traylor and his wife Liz were facing the challenges of a growing church. Pastor Traylor recognized that the needs of the church had changed over time, so he asked the music minister to resign. Given the needs of the congregation, this minister was no longer in the right place. Despite this reality, the minister was beloved by many in the church, and Pastor Traylor's decision was unpopular. An outspoken group of about twenty-five people began to call for his resignation. The months that followed were extremely difficult, and Pastor Traylor wanted to leave. He prayed, "God, I'll go to Toadsuck, Arkansas, if you'll send me there."[6] Up until this point, the Traylors had been fond of saying that they'd never had a bad day in ministry. But one evening he returned home to find three men from the church waiting for him in front of the house.

Since my own mother hailed from a farming town in Arkansas, I'm not sure I appreciate Ted's disparaging reference to that fair state. But having planted and pastored two growing churches for fifteen years, I can relate to making a tough call regarding a staff person and catching hell for it (not swearing, just tracing the source). Any leader who has sacrificed to move the ball down the field in ministry has similar war stories to tell.

Faced with the alternatives of a wimpy board that neither rewards achievement nor penalizes cheating, and a controlling board that is always there for you except when you need them, a true leader will embrace freedom with accountability any day of the week and twice on Sunday.

Supporting Pastoral Leadership

The flipside of accountability is support. This task, analogous to that of a cheerleader or even a bodyguard, is the fourth and final piece of the board's job. If the pastor is fulfilling the mission while respecting the boundaries, the pastor deserves the board's unflinching support. This support is not a kind word in private. It's the support expected by a police officer under fire who says to his or her partner, "Cover me," then breaks in to the next room. The board must have the pastor's back at all times if it expects to keep a courageous leader. Its members must agree before being allowed on the board that they will never undermine the leadership of the pastor but instead will passionately defend the pastor who is winning the game and playing within the rules. If the pastor is losing or cheating, the solution is not undermining the pastor's leadership but applying accountability instead.

Paul Borden, author of *Hit the Bullseye,* compares the board to a group of tribal elders in the rain forest. The chief of the tribe climbs the tallest tree in order to direct the establishment of the village in a new location. From this high vantage point, the chief can see the big picture and call out where to build the huts, where to plant the crops, where to post look-outs, etc. At the base of the tree stands a circle of tribal elders with long pointed spears. If the chief tries to climb down and deny the village the benefit of his guidance, they point their spears upward to send him back to his perch. If any tribespeople leave their work and try to pull the chief down, the elders turn their spears outward and send them back to their duties. That's a picture of no-nonsense accountability and support.[7]

Let's return to the story of Ted Traylor and the three men waiting for him at his house that evening. As he drew closer to them, he realized they were his friends and began to wonder if they had come to tell him it was time to go. Instead, they asked him if he remembered the story of David in hiding and the water from his hometown well in Bethlehem. They began to explain that they had gotten up early in the morning, driven to his home in North Alabama, and met his parents, who showed them the well. One of the men reached into the car and handed Pastor Traylor a jar filled with water.

> I cried. I'm not ashamed to say it. We all did. Three mighty men had brought me refreshment from my own Bethlehem. Then they drew closer and their tone was very serious. "We want to make this statement to you: we will die for our pastor. We will die for you. If you stay straight and be moral and be ethical and be biblical, we will die for you.". . . "We're not serving you, we're serving the King who called you. And we are in this together."[8]

These friends recognized that Pastor Traylor hadn't done anything immoral. He had led, just as they had asked him to do. That was the turning point. The deacons, even those who disagreed with his decision, stood with their pastor. Board members like these are few and far between. May their tribe increase.

Keeping the Board on Track

Who keeps the board focused on accountability and support rather than on leadership and management? As depicted in Figure 10.1, two officers on the board, the pastor and secretary, make vital contributions, but a third is ultimately responsible: the chairperson, whose job is to ensure that the Accountability Principles are enforced. The board does its work together; but because groups cannot lead or be held accountable, the board needs a responsible individual to see that governance happens. The pastor could govern except for one reality: In the Accountable Leadership strategy, the pastor is held accountable by the board, so the pastor as chairperson would short-circuit the monitoring of performance.

FIGURE 10.1 Three Board Officers

The secretary is a more critical officer on a *Winning on Purpose* board than on a typical board. Not only must the secretary maintain minutes and agendas, this person is the custodian of the Guiding Principles—the tool that the board uses to perform its entire job description. Think back to the four pieces of governance: 1) The board connects with the Owner and beneficiaries so that the Guiding Principles serve their interests. 2) The board composes and refreshes the Guiding Principles document. 3) The board monitors the pastor's performance using the Guiding Principles as the criteria. 4) The board supports the pastor in accordance with the Guiding Principles. So the person in charge of the Guiding Principles is indispensable. The secretary works under the chairperson, who sees that governance is done with integrity.

Finally, we come to the pastor as a board officer. This feature of Accountable Leadership is a major departure both from the "ex-officio" model in forms of congregational polity and from the Carver model. In older Baptist congregations, for example, multiple boards and standing committees are mandated in the bylaws, and the pastor is an ex-officio member of every one. While *ex-officio* properly means that the pastor is a member "by virtue of the office," some misuse the term to indicate a non-voting member. The result is a pastor who touches everything but impacts nothing. If applied to a congregation, the Carver model would exclude the pastor from board membership entirely. By contrast in the *Winning on Purpose* approach, the pastor, as the leader of the church, is not only a full member of the board, but also leads the board by taking the initiative to envision and inspire it. In practice this means the pastor will be leading the board in study of Scripture, in prayer for God's guidance, in agenda preparation—along with the other two officers, and in deliberation of the board's decisions. It does not mean the pastor gets extra votes or has the responsibility for enforcing board process. And there is one deliberation that the pastor does not lead: the annual performance review, to avoid a conflict of interest. That one must be led directly by the chairperson.

Congregations need board members who, like good tribal elders, will point spears upward at pastors who abandon their perch in the tree and will point spears at the village critics otherwise. If you know godly people who could do that but whose true ambition is for something less, such as being commissioner of the NFL, get them to keep those plans on hold. The Church needs them, and I would urge you to confirm their nomination and issue them a long, well-sharpened spear.

SUMMARY & PREVIEW

- *Governance is distinct from leadership and management.*
- *The board represents the Owner of the team.*
- *The board defines goals, boundaries, and scoring.*
- *The board keeps score and calls penalties.*
- *Good governance supports and defends leadership and management.*
- *Three board officers keep the board on track: chairperson, pastor, and secretary.*

The next chapter covers the position of management, played by the staff. Every area of ministry and operation in the congregation is overseen by a staff person, a full-time, part-time, or unpaid ministry leader heading up a major team or department. Proper function and relationship to the senior pastor, board, and congregation are covered, as well as the value of investing in staff.

Notes

1. President Bush's public announcement of Condoleezza Rice as his Secretary of State nominee on Nov. 14, 2004. www.whitehouse.gov/news/releases/2004/11/20041116-3.html (accessed on November 20, 2004).

2. Aubrey Malphurs, *Planting Growing Churches for the 21st Century: A Comprehensive Guide for New Churches and Those Desiring Renewal,* 2nd ed. (Grand Rapids: Baker, 1998), 131–49. Even if you buy my premise, you would still do well to read Malphurs' book.

3. John Carver, Boards *That Make a Difference: A New Design for Leadership in Nonprofit and Public Organizations,* 2nd ed. (San Francisco: Jossey-Bass, 1997), 120–22.

4. Matthew 16:18, Ephesians 5:25, 1 Corinthians 3:16 , 1 Peter 2:9

5. The trusteeship of the board for the interests of Christ and the intended beneficiaries of his church does not bear against the privilege and responsibility of every disciple of Christ to represent him. There is no challenge here to the priesthood of believers, simply a special application of it at the board level.

6. Condensed from "Water from Home," by Ted Traylor, *Leadership Journal,* vol. XXV, no. 4, Fall 2004, 43–45.

7. See Paul D. Borden, *Hit the Bullseye: How Denominations Can Aim the Congregation at the Mission Field,* (Nashville: Abingdon, 2003), 35–55 for a chapter entitled, "No Accountability: No Change."

8. Traylor, pp. 44–45.

CHAPTER ELEVEN
The Staff Plays Management

My main job was developing talent. I was a gardener providing
water and other nourishment to our top 750 people.
Of course, I had to pull out some weeds, too.
Jack Welch

STEVE MCQUEEN PLAYS AN ENGINE ROOM CHIEF named Jake Holman in the film Sand Pebbles, set at the beginning of China's civil war in 1926. As he walks on board the U.S.S. San Pablo, he finds it staffed with nearly as many Chinese laborers as American sailors. Each station appears to have its own servant who carries out the less desirable chores. Inside the engine room, Jake initiates changes to shape up efficiency. As he begins to do his own work, he displaces a Chinese worker who has been servicing the engine faithfully though not properly. Though technically these local servants have no business on the gunboat to begin with, a fellow naval officer rebukes Jake: "You can't take that away from him; that's his rice bowl."

Congregations, denominations, and parachurch organizations are well-stocked with underproductive staff members who are not challenged, redeployed, or let go for one simple reason: it's their rice bowl. Apart from missional accountability, staff members may be seen as an overhead expense, necessary in some degree to keep the institution alive. Or they may be seen as spiritual people who have given themselves to God's work and should therefore be supported based on their needs rather than their effectiveness. By contrast, the Accountable Leadership strategy creates a vital role for the staff as a team of top ministry equippers and mobilizers in the context of a local congregation.

Excellence of Execution

The senior pastor leads the board to ensure that it provides the congregation with good governance, i.e., establishing principles for biblical mission and boundaries, then monitoring performance against those principles. However, it is not the board that manages the actual ministry of the congregation. Just as critical as having the board in the governance position and the senior pastor in the leadership position, the staff fulfills the management position.

In the last two decades of the twentieth century, organizational writers tended—often with good reason—to downplay management in favor of leadership. "The problem with many organizations, and especially the ones that are failing, is that they tend to be over-managed and under-led. They may excel in the ability to handle the daily routine, yet never question whether the routine should be done at all."[1] Especially in times of rapid change, a ministry organization needs not just operational leadership to keep the ship on course but transformational leadership to chart new courses.

As helpful as the emphasis on leadership has been and continues to be, many ministry endeavors fail not for lack of vision but for lack of execution. We must recover a high value on management, which is just as important as leadership.

The traditional word for a manager in the English Bible is *steward*. Management and stewardship are synonyms that both refer to a trusted position that utilizes resources to accomplish what the owner of those resources desires. The first reference to a steward in Scripture is Eliezer of Damascus, who managed all the affairs of Abraham's household and possessions.[2] Jesus used the role of steward in the ancient world to teach his disciples that his expectations of them in ministry would be proportionate to what they had received:

> Who then is the faithful and wise manager, whom the master puts in charge of his servants to give them their food allowance at the proper time? It will be good for that servant whom the master finds doing so when he returns. Truly I tell you, he will put him in charge of all his possessions. But suppose the servant says to himself, "My master is taking a long time in coming," and he then begins to beat the other servants, both men and women, and to eat and drink and get drunk. The master of that servant will come on a day when he does not expect him and at an hour he is not aware of. He will cut him to pieces and assign him a place with the unbelievers. The servant who knows the master's will and does not get ready or does not do what the master wants will be beaten with many blows. But the one who does not know and does things deserving punishment will be beaten with few blows. From everyone who has been given much, much will be demanded; and from the one who has been entrusted with much, much more will be asked.[3]

A stewardship is a trusted management assignment over anything of value from people to goods to intangibles. As the apostle Paul wrote, "Think of us in this way, as servants of Christ and *stewards of God's mysteries*. Moreover, it is required of stewards that they be found trustworthy."[4] Or, in the words of the apostle Peter, "Like *good stewards of the manifold grace of God,* serve one another with whatever gift each of you has received."[5]

To expand on the vital contribution of the staff in congregations using the Accountable Leadership strategy, Table 11.1 contrasts management with both leadership and governance. Management of the ministry is entrusted to the staff, leadership of the ministry is entrusted to the senior pastor, and governance of the ministry is entrusted to the board. All are servants, each with separate and vital contributions.

While the board protects the ministry with excellence and the pastor orchestrates the ministry with excellence, the primary function of management is excellence of execution. For decades, leadership books have juxtaposed statements similar to these: Management does things right and seeks efficiency; leadership does the right things and seeks effectiveness. To these statements we may add: Governance defines what is right and seeks accountability.

TABLE 11.1 Management, Leadership, and Governance

MANAGEMENT	LEADERSHIP	GOVERNANCE
Is entrusted to the staff	Is entrusted to the pastor	Is entrusted to the board
Executes with excellence	Directs with excellence	Protects with excellence
Does things right	Does the right things	Defines what is right
Contributes efficiency	Contributes effectiveness	Contributes accountability
Answers to the pastor	Answers to the board	Answers to the church
Translates vision to action	Translates mission to vision	Articulates mission
Links pastor to ministries	Links staff to board	Links church to Owner
Operates within boundaries	Enforces boundaries	Establishes boundaries
Runs tactical operations	Runs strategic operations	Writes and monitors policy
Meets frequently	Meets with staff and board	Meets infrequently
Solves problems of today	Solves problems of tomorrow	Prioritizes the problems

Several key connections are reflected in the table. The staff answers to the pastor rather than to the board or to the congregation. We will return to this point later in the chapter. By contrast, the senior pastor answers to the board under normal circumstances, and the board answers to the church.[6] The connection of mission to action is represented by noting that the board articulates mission, the pastor translates the mission into vision (a picture of mission-accomplished within a specific context and period), and the staff translates the vision into action. Governance links the church to its Owner, the leadership of the senior pastor links the board to the staff, and the staff links the pastor to all the ministries carried out by the congregation.

In operational terms, Table 11.1 shows that the staff runs the tactical level, the pastor runs the strategic level, and the board creates and enforces broad policy affecting both levels.[7] The form and frequency of meetings follows function. The staff must coordinate frequently with each other through almost daily communications punctuated by weekly or monthly staff meetings to solve problems of today. At the other end of the spectrum, the governance group should meet infrequently in order to leave leadership and management in the capable hands of the pastor and staff. The board should keep out of management, and the staff should keep out of governance. The pastor is the only organizational link between the two.

A Comprehensive Staff

The work of the staff is all about people. Staff are trusted people who manage the work of gifted people to serve the needs of precious people who need a personal relationship with the Lord of all people. So the work matters, and the management of that work matters: "Organizations don't execute unless the right people, individually and collectively, focus on the right details at the right time."[8]

Winning on Purpose uses the term *staff* in a comprehensive and functional manner. Staff includes full-time, part-time, and unpaid ministry managers that head up every major team or department throughout the organization. Areas traditionally viewed as "spiritual," such as worship and education, are included, but so are areas that are traditionally viewed as "practical," such as facilities and finances. So the term *staff* is comprehensive not only with regard to categories of employment but also with regard to categories of activity. Each of the two kinds of categories raises a question.

Why refer to unpaid leaders of major ministries as staff? Because the responsibility, authority, and accountability attached to this level of management are the same regardless of employment factors. So-called "volunteers" managing a division of ministry are, in fact, compensated according to their effectiveness in an Accountable Leadership setting, even though compensation in the form of appreciation and fulfillment is intangible. And so-called "professionals" doing the same job are motivated by those same intangibles, in addition to their wages. Finally, the use of the word *staff* makes it easy to perceive and remember that the top ministry coordinators work as part of the pastor's team. In the United States at least, *staff* readily connotes a team directed by a primary leader.

Why put the stewards of all ministries and operations on the same level, both "spiritual" and "practical"? One reason is to break down a false separation between the two. All of God's work that human beings coordinate is spiritual in purpose, and all of it takes place in the material world. We want spiritually-minded people managing practical action that fulfills the vision of the congregation. It is not only unnecessary but also counterproductive to place facilities and finances in a separate category from the staff team led by the pastor. This separation sometimes happens through a specialized committee or board and at other times happens through direct management of finances by a treasurer on the church board. Either of these arrangements will defeat the purpose of the Accountable Leadership strategy.

Let's consider finances for each these three functions: management, leadership, and governance. How does the board fulfill its responsibility with regard to the congregation's money? It does so by *governing* the use of money in the ministry. What does it mean to govern the use of money? It means to prescribe the missional outcomes that money should be funding, to prohibit unacceptable practices for handling that money, and to monitor the outcomes and practices so the pastor can be held accountable for achieving the first and constraining the second.

Those who *manage* the use of money for the congregation, however, are not the people on the board but the people on the staff. Does this mean that the board loses control of the finances? No, the direct control is not lost but rather delegated, and the indirect control is achieved through the creation of the Guiding Principles document and the subsequent monitoring of performance vis-a-vis the Guiding Principles.

The one who ensures that the staff manages money within the purposes and boundaries established by the board is the senior pastor. In other words, the pastor *leads* the use of money for the congregation by seeing that the board sets Guiding Principles in place and seeing that the staff operates within those principles. In the Accountable Leadership strategy, there can be no confusion about whose job it is to make sure the finances are handled in a safe and effective manner. The buck quite literally stops on the desk of the senior pastor, not by ultimately setting the policies and not by ultimately applying them, but by ultimately leading those who do. The pastor who takes good care of money does not need accounting skills but leadership skills.

How many areas of ministry headed by staff should a congregation have, and which ones should they be? Naturally, that answer will vary greatly based on the size, the developmental stage, and the culture of both the congregation and the community it seeks to reach. Some of the congregation plays ministry on teams that build a strong home base, and some on teams that reach out from the home base to impact the community and beyond.

The Pastor's Team

In the Accountable Leadership strategy, the staff works for the senior pastor, not for the board or the congregation. The clearer and cleaner this line of accountability, the more secure and collaborative the staff team can become. Lines of accountability that link staff members to the board or congregation in addition to the senior pastor are nothing but fault lines that set up a congregation for division and staff members for painful conflict. When a staff member has a clearly defined responsibility, a generous freedom of authority, and a single line of accountability, he or she can run hard with confidence and purpose.

We have covered different modes of leadership for the senior pastor for each of these three arenas: board, staff, and congregation. Whereas the pastor leads the board primarily through *inspiration* and leads the congregation primarily through *teaching*, the pastor leads the staff primarily through *directing*. After leaving the board environment equipped with a few primary objectives and a few essential rules of engagement, the pastor assembles the team that will need to turn the vision into reality and works out a strategy to deploy each member of that team for his or her maximum fruitfulness.

What shape does that team take? Is it like an Olympic track and field team—a group of strong individual performers that cheer each other on but make most of their contributions separately? Is it like an American college football team, which can run successful plays only by executing together as a well-oiled machine? Is it like a baseball team that scores through an accumulation of individual hits and runs but protects its lead through intricate coordination of defense on the field? The answer is a resounding "Maybe." *The staff team must take whatever shape its leader believes will help the congregation achieve its mission while respecting its values.* The reason the leader gets to decide this is simple: the leader is the one who will be held accountable for the performance of the team as a whole. Wise senior pastors know and deploy themselves where they can make the best personal contribution to the congregation's success; then they develop other leaders and help them deploy where they can contribute best. The shape of the staff team will change dramatically as the church grows to keep ministry decentralized yet accountable through empowered leaders and servants.

Some lead pastors will not be the ones to generate the brightest and boldest initiatives but will instead coax them forth from a highly collaborative team that they have nurtured. Others will be natural visionaries and will bring well-formed strategies to a looser, more independently minded team for their refinement and application. There is no one right pattern or profile. It does not matter exactly *how* the team wins. What matters is how *big* they win, and whether they do so without "cheating," i.e. violating the Boundary Principles.

Regardless of tradition or polity, and sometimes regardless of whether they publicly deny it, all larger congregations are led to breakthroughs and sustained periods of growth by strong senior pastors backed by strong teams of winners on their staff. A congregation or board that underestimates this direct relationship may discount the significance of a winning staff and settle for far less of an impact on the community than they might otherwise make for God's Kingdom.

Accountable Leadership avoids the dysfunctional hiring and firing of staff by making clear to everyone that the pastor is authorized to make any decision regarding staff aimed at better fulfilling the mission as long as that decision does not violate the board's Boundary Principles.

Two Degrees of Separation

Maintaining healthy accountability for the staff requires that certain functions and players be separated from each other. For the staff to have appropriate freedom for action, it is important to keep the board and its members—except for the senior pastor—apart from the management function. For the board to have appropriate freedom for evaluation, it is equally important to keep the staff and its members—except for the senior pastor—apart from the governance function. The leadership linkage provided by the senior pastor is the only healthy crossover position between the two teams. So the position of senior pastor not only links the board and staff to each other, but it also separates them from each other by two degrees. The board is there to govern, the pastor is there to lead, and the staff is there to manage. Thus, the board maintains one degree of separation from leading the congregation and two degrees of separation from managing its ministries. In the other direction, the staff is positioned one step away from leading the congregation and two steps away from governing its policies.

Allowing top-level staff or their immediate family on the board creates dysfunction. This dysfunction is not a result of the *personality* of the individuals involved—though personality can be a separate source—but is instead a result of the *positioning* of those individuals. When an associate pastor or any other top staff member is placed on the governing board of the church, a conflict of interest is created. The senior pastor may believe that another pastor on the board will serve as a special advocate and ally. That expectation may or may not be realized, but in either case accountability is disfigured beyond all recognition. In stressful circumstances, a pastor simply cannot be expected to hold a staff member accountable at the office and then walk into the boardroom to be held accountable by the same individual. Under these conditions, people will play games, but no one will win in the long run.

This dysfunction will arise whether there is one staff person on the board or more than one. It will also arise if a close family member either of a staff person or the senior pastor is placed on the board. No matter how circumspect such a board member may be, the dysfunction will be unavoidable in one of three ways: 1) the board member will advocate for a special interest, 2) the board member will overcompensate and unfairly disadvantage that interest, or 3) the board member will act with neutrality, but other staff and board members will assume him or her to be biased and will alter their behavior in response.

Smaller congregations with one or two families of special influence may find it difficult to transition to an Accountable Leadership strategy in terms of the two degrees of separation required. Nevertheless, it is important to move as quickly as possible away from overlapping board and staff members and families. There is a vital role of service for each and every qualified leader in the church. A person may either govern or manage, and he or she may even do both in different years. But a person may not both govern and manage the ministries of the church during the same annual cycle and still preserve the heart of Accountable Leadership.

Investment, Not Expense

The congregation that wants a winning staff must put a high proportion of its money into securing and supporting them. However, this process is not expensive. In fact, it is not an expense at all. The right staff members are an investment rather than an expense. I once heard a leading pastor relate his standard response when the occasional critic would complain about staff support comprising more than fifty percent of the church budget: "I want to apologize for that. I wish it could be 100% that we invest in people instead of other necessities, but we just haven't figured out how to get it up that high!"

Please don't misunderstand this point. I am not playing with words when I assert that the right staff people are not an expense, and I am not talking about them as a spiritual investment—though of course they are that as well. No, I mean quite literally that the right people on the staff do not cost money. Why not? Because they add more value to the congregation in both spiritual and material resources than the congregation spends to support them. If they don't, then we have the wrong people, or else we have the right people in the wrong places.

Spiritual value is added to the congregation in a multitude of ways. Material value is added to the congregation by effective staff in two particular ways. First, effective staff leaders go beyond maintaining existing ministries in order to create and develop new ones that reach more people from the community. Second, effective staffers work less as doers and more as equippers, mobilizing the people of the church to invest themselves more deeply and fruitfully in service to others. More people and more highly invested people both inevitably lead to more resources to support the work of the congregation.

We have defined staff without regard to employment status. However, a couple of compensation questions naturally arise: Who should we pay for their work in the church? How much should we pay them? Here are six simple principles, consistent with both Scripture and the Accountable Leadership strategy:

1) Full-time pastors who lead with excellent results should be conspicuously honored through generous compensation.

2) Laborers are worthy of their wages, so it is never wrong to pay full-value for something that needs to be done in the church.

3) Followers of Christ are expected to give their time, abilities, and finances to God's work, so it is never wrong to accept someone's gift of service to the church without recompense.

4) Whenever possible, a staff addition should be designed to multiply and mobilize volunteers in ministry, not to replace one.

5) Compensation should be fair and flexible (not formulaic), starting at the level needed to bring the right person on board and rising to incentivize the accomplishment of mission goals.

6) Unpaid staff leaders should be rewarded for their achievements both intangibly through forms of recognition that they value and tangibly through the best training and resources available.

The "proper care and feeding" of staff—both paid and unpaid—will require new patterns as a congregation grows. In a small church below 200 in attendance, the pastor should have no problem personally overseeing half a dozen or so top-level volunteer and part-time staff. In a very large church over 800, many lead pastors do well to work through another chief of staff, such as an executive pastor. In between those sizes, the senior pastor may have a small team of associate pastors who in turn oversee the rest of the staff for the most part. The cultural sensibilities of the congregation will determine how business-like or how relational these patterns become. All that Accountable Leadership requires is that every team has a leader and that every team leader directly or indirectly works for the senior pastor, who must give account to the board for the big picture.

In a congregation that wins on purpose, staff plays an essential position: the management of ministries through which members of the congregation can best use their God-given abilities to reach those who need Christ and to care for those who know him. Therefore, people are not kept on staff because it's their rice-bowl, but because it's the congregation's best investment for a greater harvest.

SUMMARY & PREVIEW

- *The function of management is excellence of execution.*

- *"Staff" includes all top-level ministry heads regardless of compensation.*

- *The staff works for the senior pastor, not for the board or the congregation.*

- *Allowing top-level staff or immediate family on the board creates dysfunction.*

- *The right staff is an investment rather than an expense.*

Part Four covers the equipment needed to implement Accountable Leadership. Each congregation plays the game in a league of its own in terms of polity, and each needs to master the use of schedules. However, before we get to either of those tools, we begin our final section with a chapter on the best use of organizational documents to win on purpose.

Notes

1. Warren Bennis and Burt Nanus, *Leaders: The Strategies for Taking Charge*, (New York: Harper & Row, 1985), 21.
2. Genesis 15:2
3. Luke 12: 42–48, TNIV
4. 1 Corinthians 4:1–2, NRSV. Emphasis added.
5. 1 Peter 4:10, NRSV. Emphasis added.
6. For an explanation of who owns the church, see "Trustees for Whom" in chapter 10.
7. These operations empower the congregation for ministry to the community and each other, which Figure 3.4 depicts as the reason the rest of the organization exists.
8. Larry Bossidy and Ram Charan, *Execution: The Discipline of Getting Things Done*, (New York: Crown Business, 2002), 33.

DO WE HAVE
THE RIGHT EQUIPMENT?

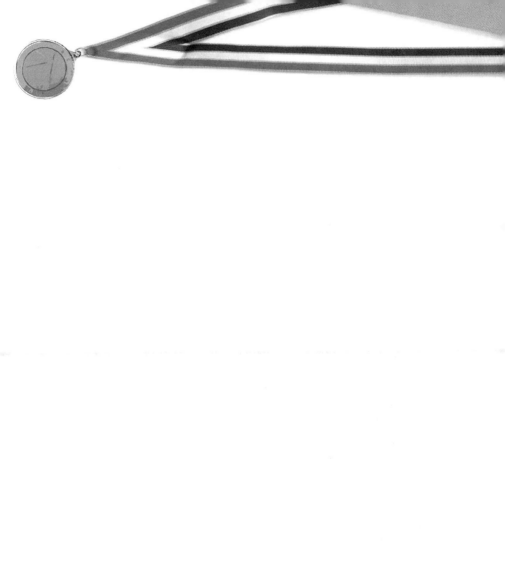

CHAPTER TWELVE
Organizational Documents
Set Up the Game

The winds of God are always blowing, but you must set the sails.
Unknown

CHILDREN READ AN ORGANIZATIONAL DOCUMENT every time they play a new board game or video game. In ancient times—just prior to Pong, Atari, and Pac-Man—this organizational document was always printed inside the lid of the box. Whether Monopoly, Chutes and Ladders, or Scrabble, there under the box-top in concise terms were found the same elements that comprise the Accountable Leadership strategy: Object of the Game, Rules for Play, and How to Keep Score. Video gamers get the same information onscreen but with cool sound effects.

Writing and reading church organizational documents is no more a part of doing ministry than reading the box-top is a part of playing Parcheesi. But, it is no less a part either. We need those guidelines to understand the game up front and to answer questions as they arise. So without further nostalgia, let's explore the right documentary equipment for the Accountable Leadership strategy.

Creating a Corporate "Pair o' Docs"

Just as many congregations of the first century were organized as synagogues, many congregations of the twenty-first century in Western cultures are organized as corporations. Neither vessel is biblical in origin, but both are indigenous to their culture and adaptable to the biblical mission of the church. American nonprofit corporations utilize a pair of primary organizational documents: the *articles of incorporation* and the *bylaws*. Simply put, the articles are used to create the corporation, and the bylaws are used to operate it.

Table 12.1 presents eight specific goals that the articles of incorporation should be designed to accomplish.

TABLE 12.1 Goals for the Articles of Incorporation

1) To create and name a nonprofit corporation in accordance with state law

2) To satisfy requirements for tax exemption at the state and federal level

3) To fix the purpose of the corporation as a healthy, growing, and reproducing congregation

4) To identify the corporation with its denomination or movement

5) To leave maximum flexibility for organizational structures and strategies

6) To include basic legal provisions that limit the liability of the congregation and its personnel

7) To fix the distribution of assets back to the denomination or movement in case of corporate dissolution

8) To specify how to amend the articles of incorporation

The articles should say no more than is necessary to accomplish these goals. There are two main reasons for this brevity: 1) articles of incorporation tend to wind up deeply stored and rarely consulted, and 2) articles of incorporation must be filed with the state for a fee and refiled for a fee whenever they are amended.

My colleagues in Canada, Australia, and New Zealand tell me that similar organizational documents are required in Commonwealth countries. However, the need for articles of incorporation is for some congregations removed by an act of parliament that establishes the legal status of its denomination. Also, the tax laws pertaining to religious corporations are quite different outside the United States, as are the historical relationships of church and state.

Clarity about the Bylaws

In older congregations, the articles or the bylaws are often called the church "constitution." In the legal community, this term is not used for nonprofit corporations. The verb *constitute* might more naturally apply to creating a legal entity through the articles of incorporation. On the other hand, the constitutions of nations are analogous to the bylaws of corporations. Adding to the confusion, some congregations combine the articles and bylaws into a single document (generally not a good idea) and refer to it as their constitution. For all these reasons, the term "constitution" is generally best discarded for the sake of clarity.

Beyond terminology, we must be clear about just who is speaking to whom through the bylaws. This document properly expresses the intent of the congregation, not the board, the pastor, or the denomination. Even in traditions of polity without a voting church membership, the bylaws should be composed in the voice of the body as a whole by whoever is authorized to speak for it. Despite whatever role the board may play in drafting or approving the document, the bylaws are addressed primarily *to* the board in order to grant it legitimate authority to govern within specified parameters. In short, the bylaws are how the congregation authorizes the board to be the board.

Why not simply authorize the board through the articles of incorporation and forgo bylaws for the sake of simplicity? While this would be legal for a U.S. nonprofit corporation, it would create an unwelcome dilemma: either the organizational strategy would be prescribed in the articles or it would be left to the board to prescribe for itself. The first alternative fails to facilitate continuous flexibility and improvement since articles are less likely to be revised—a poor choice for adaptation to constant change. The second alternative minimizes the accountability of the board to anyone outside itself since it would define not only the parameters of the pastor and staff but also the parameters of its own authority.[1] For American congregations organizing as nonprofit organizations, therefore, it is recommended that the articles, in order to preserve maximum freedom for improvement and reinvention, should not even reference an organizational model, whereas the bylaws should clearly prescribe one. So, a congregation using *Winning on Purpose* would utilize the bylaws to make the Accountable Leadership strategy official.

What the Bylaws Need to Cover

The more bureaucratic the congregation, the more what-ifs its bylaws attempt to solve in advance. By contrast, the Accountable Leadership strategy stresses trust, flexibility, results, and clarity—all of which generally translate into brevity, perhaps 4–6 pages. Nevertheless, there are a number of essential points that the bylaws should address. Table 12.2 contains a list of irreducible goals for bylaws designed to implement Accountable Leadership fully as presented in *Winning on Purpose*. The wording of the document may vary from one context to another, but any provision that does not achieve one of these stated goals is superfluous and best left out.

TABLE 12.2 Goals for the Bylaws

1) To provide an effective organizational structure subject to annual revision

2) To describe the church's commitment to historical Christian orthodoxy

3) To describe the church's participation with its denomination or movement

4) To describe the mission as outward in terms of the Great Commission

5) To specify an organizational model that keeps the roles of senior pastor, board, staff, and congregation distinct and effective

6) To define the senior pastor as the leader of the church both spiritually and organizationally

7) To define the board as a governing team, supporting the pastor's leadership

8) To define the staff, paid or unpaid, as the managers of all ministry operations and as working for the senior pastor

9) To define the congregation as a body of believers who are committed to the mission of the church and who carry out the ministries of the church

10) To list certain major decisions that require congregational support

11) To include additional legal provisions that limit the liability of the church and its personnel

12) To specify how to amend the various parts of the bylaws

How the Bylaws Need to Be Changed

Newsflash: the bylaws are not the Bible. It's okay to change them whenever they can be improved or need to be replaced. Three pieces of advice follow for making these changes well:

Review the bylaws each and every year for potential revisions. Good bylaws are more like tailfins than spoilers. They provide stability in flight, not resistance to take-off. The congregation that grows accustomed to leaders suggesting minor annual updates will be prepared to consider more substantial revisions to the bylaws when they are needed. Otherwise, the mere mention of changing the bylaws may provoke anxiety. So go ahead, even if it's just swapping a semicolon for a period—or, if it's been a while, swapping a *ye* for a *you*—tweak the document once a year.

Employ each player of the Accountable Leadership strategy in the process. The pastor is there to lead. So, Pastor, lead the process and make sure the new bylaws are the best they can be to set up the church for success. The board is there to govern. So, Board, monitor the leadership of the pastor in this process to make sure that current boundaries are being respected. The staff is there to manage. So, Staff, execute the details of the process as directed to make sure the final product is excellent. The congregation is there to minister. So, Congregation, let the leadership know what you need to be more effective in reaching out to newcomers and caring for one another, then support upgrades to the bylaws that your leaders believe will help them to equip you better to do so.

Do not use a revision of the bylaws to introduce Accountable Leadership. Switching directly from traditional bylaws to Accountable Leadership bylaws may be tempting, but it is normally a mistake. Experience has proven this tactic to be counterproductive for the following reasons:

1) Whatever degree of resistance is present already will be increased because the change feels permanent yet unproven.

2) There will be pressure to water down the wording of the new document to make it more familiar and palatable.

3) If growth is not forthcoming in the short-run, the congregation may revert more deeply than ever to its old patterns and be inoculated against future attempts at systemic change.

4) Time and energy needed to demonstrate success in mission is squandered on a piece of paper.

Chapter 13 includes a transition plan that has proven effective in moving from a traditional church structure to a mission-driven accountability structure. I recommend that you follow it rather than expend unnecessary leadership capital on an organizational document.

An Aside for Unincorporated Congregations

Congregations opting not to incorporate for philosophical or strategic reasons will not need articles and bylaws as legal documents but may find it beneficial to compose some alternative kind of charter to witness both the nature of their formation and the pattern of their function. If a congregation is unwilling to define its form and function at all, it will benefit little from Accountable Leadership or any other organizational strategy. Table 12.3 contains a list of goals that might guide the composition of a charter document designed to implement Accountable Leadership in an unincorporated congregation.

TABLE 12.3 Goals for an Unincorporated Charter

1) To name the congregation

2) To define the organizational vehicle or concept for the congregation, such as an association, a house church, or a monastic community

3) To fix the purpose of the organization as a healthy, growing, and reproducing congregation

4) To note the legal and financial implications and necessities inherent in the chosen organizational vehicle or concept

5) To provide an effective organizational structure subject to revision

6) To describe the congregation's commitment to historical Christian orthodoxy

7) To describe the congregation's participation with its denomination or movement

8) To describe the mission as outward in terms of the Great Commission

9) To specify an organizational model that keeps the roles of lead pastor, governing team (functional equivalent to a board), staff, and congregation distinct and effective

10) To define the pastor as the leader of the church both spiritually and organizationally

11) To define the board equivalent as a governing team, supporting the pastor's leadership

12) To define the staff, paid or unpaid, as the managers of all ministry operations and as working for the lead pastor

13) To define the congregation as a body of believers who are committed to the mission of the church and who carry out the ministries of the church

14) To list any major decisions that require congregational support

15) To include additional legal provisions that limit the liability of the congregation's and its personnel

16) To specify how the charter may be revised as needed

How Guiding Principles Authorize the Pastor

Once the board is properly authorized through the bylaws to play its governance position, the next logical step is authorizing the pastor to play the position of leadership. Setting up all four of the key positions, the bylaws unequivocally identify the pastor as the leader of the church. However, there remains the need for the board and the pastor to agree together on the three elements that make a game worth playing: the object, the rules, and the scoring.

After the pastor leads the board through prayerful consideration of these three elements, the board's conclusions are written into a document called the Guiding Principles. This concise paper is the primary tool the board uses to provide meaningful accountability to the pastor on behalf of the church; it is not a document composed or approved by the congregation. Table 12.4 displays the three sections of the Guiding Principles along with how they compare in form and content.

TABLE 12.4 Three Sections of Guiding Principles

MISSION PRINCIPLES	BOUNDARY PRINCIPLES	ACCOUNTABILITY PRINCIPLES
Object of the Game	Rules of the Game	How to Keep Score
Responsibility	Authority	Accountability
Ends	Means	Oversight
Board speaks to Pastor	Board speaks to Pastor	Board speaks to Chair
Prescription Language	Prohibition Language	Process Language
Where are we going?	How ~~will~~ won't we get there?	Are we there yet?

The first section of Guiding Principles, and by far the most important, is called the Mission Principles. These principles define the object of the game, the responsibility of the pastor, the ends to be achieved. The next section, Boundary Principles, sets out the rules of the game, the authority of the pastor (i.e., anything within the boundaries is preauthorized), the limitations on acceptable means. Finally, the Accountability Principles describe how the board will keep score, the accountability of the pastor, and the procedures for oversight.

In addition to the comparisons above regarding the content and purpose of each section, it is also vital to analyze the recipient and form. In the Mission Principles, the board is speaking to the senior pastor in prescriptive language, defining positively what outcomes are expected. In the Boundary Principles the board is again speaking to the senior pastor but in the language of prohibition, defining in negative terms what kinds of methods are out of bounds. In the Accountability Principles, the board is not speaking to the pastor; it is speaking to its own chairperson, describing in the language of process (whether positively or negatively) the duties and procedures of the board.

The remainder of this chapter will take each section of the Guiding Principles, one at a time, and provide instructions and examples for how to compose them. The essential purpose of each section might best be understood in terms of the question that it addresses. Mission Principles: Where are we going? Boundary Principles: How will we get there? Or more precisely, how *won't* we get there? Accountability Principles: Are we there yet?

Constructing the Guiding Principles

The pastor and board have prayed, searched the Scriptures, studied the community, and deliberated among themselves. There is substantial consensus on the purpose, the ethics, and the oversight of the ministry. But then a blank sheet of paper or an empty computer screen stares back. How does a church formulate and record the principles that will clearly communicate this consensus? Let's begin with four standards that apply to all three sections: Guiding Principles should be written. And they should be concise, broad, and handy.

Writing down the principles is absolutely essential; here's the rule: if it's not written down, the board didn't say it. "Wait a minute," one might object. "Do we really have to be so formal about this communication? Can't we just talk it over and move ahead based with a shared sense of values on these matters?" In some cultures and eras, the answer may be yes. In developed nations of the 21st century, the answer is no. If you live in a society where you would buy or sell your family's home based on a handshake rather than a contract, then you can go verbal with Accountable Leadership—otherwise you need a pencil. Writing the principles down forces the board to speak with one voice, to remember what it said, and to have a single reference point available for anyone in the organization that needs to understand its intentions.

The written principles should be both concise and broad. This combination means that each of the three sections begins with one sentence that covers the entire scope of principles in that section. Believe it or not, after those three sentences are written properly, the board and the pastor have everything they need to make the Accountable Leadership strategy work. However, I recommend that boards work in two to three levels of specificity for each section of the Guiding Principles: The single sentence at the top is the *comprehensive* level for that section. It is wise to add a second tier of specificity under each comprehensive principle, which we'll call the *component* level. All the component principles of a section taken together cover exactly the same ground as the comprehensive principle for that section but with greater specificity. Under some, but not all, component principles it may be helpful to add a third tier of sentences: the detail level. The *detail* principles have the same relationship to their component principle as the component principles have to their comprehensive principle.

Finally, the Guiding Principles document should be handy. It should literally be at hand for each board member at every meeting in its current revision. (When to revise is treated in the next chapter.) The Guiding Principles are to the board members and the senior pastor what the hammer is to the carpenter and what the baton is to the conductor.

Mission Principles

We have already established that Mission Principles should define the object of the game. So how does the board, with the inspirational leadership of the pastor, write a good mission principle? First of all, be sure to address results and not means. The mission of the church is not a set of activities, even holy activities. It is an outcome: the making of disciples. No how-to's are allowed in the Mission Principles. It's all about the fruit. Second, be sure the board is addressing the senior pastor. The purpose of the Mission Principles is to prescribe the pastor's responsibility. These sentences tell the pastor what specific outcomes will constitute success for the congregation, and therefore success for the pastor's performance evaluation. While the pastor is a member of the board, even a leading member, the board speaks only as a collective governance body with a single voice and only to the pastor, as the single designated leader held responsible for the performance of the entire staff.

Table 12.5 presents four examples of a comprehensive Mission Principle. Three of them are deficient in one respect or another. Only one of them meets the three criteria of a complete mission statement that we will explain below, but first read over the examples and see if you can intuitively sense which ones are missing something.

TABLE 12.5 Comprehensive Mission Principle Examples

Example A	The mission of Gospel Chapel is to provide a Christian witness to families in northeast Atlanta until Jesus returns to gather His saints.
Example B	Coastal Community Church wants thousands of professionals and their friends in Ocean County to become fully devoted followers of Christ.
Example C	The Gathering was set up so more people every year can start exploring and experiencing God in an atmosphere of acceptance and love.
Example D	The Church of St. Andrew intends to glory God by connecting the affluent and underprivileged of Center City in Christian community.

Feeling confused? bemused? abused? The ambiguity in the examples was intentional to demonstrate the need for a useful set of criteria. Here it is. A complete mission principle should answer three questions:

1) What change are we trying to effect?

2) To what extent are we trying to effect a change?

3) For whom are we trying to effect a change?

Now take a fresh look at the table.

Example B is the only one that gives a real answer to each of these three questions. *To become fully devoted followers of Christ* represents a real change. *Thousands* communicates a degree of change. *Professionals and their friends in Ocean County* identifies for whom the change is intended. So this example is complete with regard to the criteria, regardless of how one sees the choices and composition.

Example A identifies the intended beneficiaries (*families in northeast Atlanta*) and a measure of extent (*until Jesus returns*); however no real change is stated. The words, *provide a gospel witness*, might represent change for an unreached people group somewhere but not for northeast Atlanta, where there are already hundreds of organized witnesses to the gospel.

Example C states a meaningful change (*start exploring and experiencing God*) and offers a measurable extent (*more people every year*), but it fails to tell us what people are in mind. This omission matters regardless of whether a church defines its primary ministry group broad or narrow. Technically, The Gathering could fulfill its undirected mission by paying for people on the other side of the country to attend spiritual retreat centers, making no impact on any segment of its own community.

You can deduce that the piece missing from Example D is the extent of change. We can know that connecting people in Christian community is the change and that the affluent and underprivileged of Center City are the target groups. What we don't know is how far this mission needs to go to be a success. Will two or three from each group satisfy the board? Will two or three hundred? We can't tell.

Bottom line: if a board writes a mission principle that tells the pastor what results the board wants, and if the pastor can figure out from reading it *what difference* is made *for whom* and *to what extent,* then it is a complete statement. The choice of content is up to the board under the authority of God's Word applied to the needs of a specific context, but the content should answer the three questions above.

Boundary Principles

Earlier we covered the concept of boundaries. As a quick review, here are the main points from that discussion:

- *Keeping the rules is not the object of the game.*
- *Boundaries tell you how not to play.*
- *Anything within the rules is fair game.*
- *Breaking the rules gets you a penalty.*
- *Sometimes the rules change.*

If any of these concepts are unclear to you, you can reread the details in chapter 5. At this point, however, let's move on to the process for properly composing the Boundary Principles.

Because boundaries are intended solely to mark off unacceptable behavior, they are stated in negative language. The form is prohibition, but the effect is freedom. Be on guard for any drift toward stating a boundary in positive language. With one foot on that slope, it is only a matter of time until the Boundary Principles slip down into a set of Standard Operating Procedures prescribed by the board. SOPs are perfect for operating nuclear power plants, where a value on creativity and freedom to fail would be overrated, but they are death-by-regulation for a missional congregation.

One of the most common questions about constructing boundaries as prohibitions is this: "How can we possibly anticipate all the things that might go wrong and write a rule against each one in advance?" The question answers itself, of course—you can't. So how can you keep the church protected from abuse of authority in the absence of a traditional approval system? As with Mission and Accountability Principles, the boundaries we codify will begin with a single *comprehensive* sentence. It is worded broadly enough to cover any and all unacceptable practices. Once that sentence is in place, we can break it down into component principles, any of which can also be broken down into details if necessary. However, it is the Comprehensive Boundary Principle, not the components and details underneath it, that provides us with full coverage for every situation.

While most church leaders would find a comprehensive mission statement to be somewhat familiar ground, a comprehensive boundary statement is new territory for most. However, there is nothing complex about it. Table 12.6 contains the template principle that I use for training and consulting with church boards as well as a list of topics for component principles that could be composed underneath it.

TABLE 12.6 Comprehensive Boundary Principle + Topics

Comprehensive Boundary Principle	BP 1.0	The senior pastor shall not cause or allow any practice, activity, decision, or organizational circumstance that is unlawful, imprudent, unethical, or unbiblical.
Topics for Component Boundary Principles	BP1.1	Biblical Integrity
	BP1.2	Budget Planning
	BP1.3	Financial Management
	BP1.5	Constituent Relations
	BP1.6	Staff Compensation
	BP1.7	Staff Relations
	BP1.8	Board Relations
	BP1.9	Leadership Succession

BP 1.0 is exceedingly broad, isn't it? Yes. Is it so broad as to be useless? Just the opposite. The statement must cover *every kind* of practice in the

ministry that the board would want to hold the pastor accountable to avoid or correct. And it does. However, it also reminds the board that if a reasonable person might consider a given practice to be neither unlawful, imprudent, unethical, nor unbiblical, the board has no legitimate basis for challenging that practice; it has been preauthorized by the board through its placement of the boundaries.[2]

I normally recommend that boards compose their boundaries within the top two tiers of comprehensive and component principles. A third level of detail principles may suggest or reinforce a lack of trust in the pastor's leadership. One must ask, "If it's legal, prudent, ethical, and biblical, why wouldn't we trust our pastor to decide about it?" The component level, however, is helpful to both the pastor and the board in order to pre-interpret the comprehensive statement as areas of concern while preserving a great deal of flexibility on the details.

Accountability Principles

Theoretically it would be possible for you to gain a thorough understanding of the principles of the internal combustion engine, pass a written driver's license examination with a perfect score, and still not be able to drive a car across town. Why not? Because you still have to learn simple operating procedures such as where to insert the ignition key, how to tell the brake pedal from the accelerator, and which doo-hickey turns on the windshield wipers. The same is true of operating the Accountable Leadership strategy. While the board should never impose operating procedures on the pastor, staff, or congregation, it must impose such procedures on itself in order to function. In other words, the board has to decide how it is going to do its work with integrity.

TABLE 12.7 Comprehensive Accountability Principle + Outline

Comprehensive Accountability Principle	AP 1.0	The responsibility of this board to God on behalf of people in our community who need Christ and those who have joined with us to reach them is to see that this congregation, through the leadership of its senior pastor: 1) achieves the fulfillment of its Mission Principles, and 2) avoids the violation of its Boundary Principles.

Outline for Component and Detail Accountability Principles	AP1.1	Connecting with Christ and Those He Calls Us to Serve
		AP1.1.1 Community Research and Relations
		AP1.1.2 Church Feedback and Assessment
		AP1.1.3 Devotion to Prayer and God's Word
	AP1.2	Disciplining the Process of the Board
		AP1.2.1 Board Style
		AP1.2.2 Board Job Description
		AP1.2.3 Board Member Code of Conduct
		AP1.2.4 Senior Pastor as Officer for Vision
		AP1.2.5 Chairperson as Officer for Process
		AP1.2.6 Secretary as Officer for Documentation
		AP1.2.7 Use of Board Committees
		AP1.2.8 Cost of Governance
	AP1.3	Monitoring the Performance of the Senior Pastor
		AP1.3.1 Unity of Control
		AP1.3.2 Accountability of the Senior Pastor
		AP1.3.3 Delegation to the Senior Pastor
		AP1.3.4 Performance of the Senior Pastor
		AP1.3.5 Annual Goals of the Senior Pastor
		AP1.3.6 Annual Review of the Senior Pastor

Fortunately, the board has an officer assigned to keep it on track with regard to its job—the chairperson. So there is no need to write down every procedure—just enough to give the chairperson some appropriate parameters. These parameters are called the Accountability Principles. Table 12.7 contains a sample comprehensive accountability statement followed by an outline for components and details. The outline is organized around the three accountabilities that concern the board: 1) the board's accountability to Christ and those he calls it to serve, 2) the board's accountability to itself for integrity of process, and 3) the senior pastor's accountability to the board.

It lies beyond the scope of the present volume to provide and explain all the content that might be included in the Articles of Incorporation, the Bylaws, and the Guiding Principles documents for a congregation using Winning on Purpose. There is neither sufficient print space nor mind space to do even one set of such documents justice, let alone the variety of editions required for different legal jurisdictions, ecclesiastical traditions, and mission fields. However, all of the essentials to play fair and win on purpose are right here in a box-top edition.

SUMMARY & PREVIEW

- *At the right time, and not before, the bylaws authorize the board to govern in accordance with the Accountable Leadership strategy.*

- *Through Guiding Principles that are written, concise, broad, and handy, the board authorizes the pastor to lead.*

- *Mission Principles establish the object of the game by prescribing to the pastor.*

- *Boundary Principles establish the rules of the game by proscribing to the pastor.*

- *Accountability Principles explain the scoring of the game to the chairperson of the board.*

The next chapter moves from documentary equipment to chronological equipment: when to do what for the Accountable Leadership strategy. There we will address the annual calendar, the meeting agenda, the training course, and the transition plan. All the equipment a team needs to be right—on time.

Notes

1. Chapter 2 and chapter 14 note some dysfunctional tendencies of board-dominated congregations.
2. The section titled "Interpretation and Application" in chapter 6 covers the use of this reasonable person test, which is applied routinely in courts of law.

CHAPTER THIRTEEN

Schedules Keep the Game in Play

> *Eighty percent of success is showing up.*
> Woody Allen

KIWIS AND AUSSIES LIKE TO MAKE FUN OF AMERICAN FOOTBALL, or *grid-iron*, as they call it—that is, when they're not making fun of each other. My friends down under have two favorite points of derision: American football players are wimps for wearing all that protective gear and are lazy for stopping the play with each down. By the way, it's easy to spot a retired football player from New Zealand or Australia when he's making these jokes. He looks like a retired American boxer.

One thing that all of these sporting events have in common is the very fact of being *events*, that is, things that happen in a segment of time. Games are played in real time. If you want to win, you have to know what to do with that time. Quarters, periods, downs, innings, rounds—these are all pieces of chronological equipment to keep the game in play.

Winning congregations also need chronological equipment to keep the game of mission in play. Board members who try to implement the Accountable Leadership strategy by truly governing may instead slip into old habits of approval-granting and surrogate management unless they are equipped when they walk into the meeting room to answer one question: So what happens now? This chapter offers four scheduling tools to answer that question: the annual calendar, the meeting agenda, the training and selection process, and the transition plan.

The Influence of the Annual Calendar

Traditional congregations typically hold a monthly board meeting. The board members are too busy to meet weekly, and too much church activity happens to meet less often than monthly and still hope to manage it. However, in the Accountable Leadership strategy, the board does not even *try* to manage what's happening. That's why a church has staff. The board invests its precious time and energy to govern the big picture. To leverage that investment, I recommend that church boards hold their regular meetings on a quarterly basis. Boards can still call a special meeting if an action is both necessary and urgent. And they can act upon less important urgencies by telephone, email, or video conference. By contrast, the staff should meet far more frequently—weekly and/or monthly—in order to function as the center of ministry coordination. There are several reasons for quarterly board meetings under normal circumstances:

1) Meeting more often than necessary tempts a board to manage rather than govern.

2) Meeting less often than necessary tempts a board to abdicate rather than govern.

3) Most boards will govern most effectively by holding two to six carefully prepared meetings each year.

4) The staff should meet much more often than the board to coordinate the details of management.

The annual calendar in Table 13.1 keeps the board playing governance, rather than management, with quarterly meetings. Theoretically, each meeting could engage all parts of the board's job. However, the dedicated-focus calendar brings two benefits to governance in depth: a larger block of time for each major deliberation, and a singular concentration of preparation between meetings.

In this calendar model, the board for the new fiscal year dedicates its first quarterly meeting to connecting with Christ, the Owner of the organization for whose interests it has just become a representative. The focus of this meeting is on prayer and searching the Scriptures for wisdom to govern well. The pastor uses the training portion of the meeting to cover biblical mission and values that the board needs for unity of purpose. The parts of the board's job description (other than connecting with Christ) are reviewed briefly, primarily in reference to the focus and preparation of future meetings. These parts are: connecting with people to be served, monitoring the performance of the senior pastor, and updating the Guiding Principles.

TABLE 13.1 Calendar Model for Quarterly Board Meetings

Meeting	Focus	Training	Status Check
1st Quarter	Connecting with Christ	Biblical Mission and Values	• Connecting with People • Updating the Principles • Monitoring Performance
2nd Quarter	Connecting with People	Culture and Community	• Updating the Principles • Monitoring Performance • Connecting with Christ
3rd Quarter	Updating the Principles	Accountability and Support	• Monitoring Performance • Connecting with Christ • Connecting with People
4th Quarter	Monitoring Performance	Leadership Development	• Connecting with Christ • Connecting with People • Updating the Principles

The second quarter is invested in connecting with the people to be served by the ministry, with a primary emphasis on people in the community and a supporting emphasis on caring for needs within the existing congregation. This focus requires reliable data, both quantitative and qualitative, from those who know how to gather and interpret it. If someone on the board has these skills, great. Otherwise, appoint or hire a competent resource person for this occasion. The training piece, whether done personally by the pastor or by bringing in a presenter, educates the board on the culture and community it wants to reach. As in every meeting, the remaining governance tasks are reviewed, starting with the one scheduled for the next meeting.

The third quarter focuses on reviewing and revising the Guiding Principles. This timing fits because the board has its judgment informed by the connecting work of its first two meetings. Training relates to the board's work of governance: supporting and holding the pastor account-able for fruitful leadership. Other board tasks are also reviewed.

The board's fourth and final meeting of the year revolves around monitoring the pastor's performance. This check of goals achieved and boundaries respected coincides with preparation of the next year's budget—including pastoral compensation.[1] Training is provided for leadership development. Other board duties are reviewed in the context of a new board coming on for the year ahead.

Proportions of the Meeting Agenda

Now to the nuts and bolts of the board meeting: Who will lead us? Who will participate? How will the agenda be prepared?

The answer to the first question is that the officers of the board will lead it through the process. The senior pastor sets the spiritual tone, presents training, and leads the focus portion of the meeting with one exception: the review of pastoral performance in the fourth quarter. The chairperson leads this fourth quarter focus on performance, conducts the quarterly review of governance tasks, and throughout the entire meeting enforces compliance with the Accountability Principles. The secretary provides advance materials to the board members, a current revision of the Guiding Principles at each seat during the meeting, and, after the conclusion of the meeting, a record of board actions taken.

Those who attend and participate in the meeting are the current board members, including the three officers above, plus any staff member or resource person that is needed to provide pertinent information for the board's use. Others should generally not be invited to attend a board meeting because of the human tendency to seek a consensus of all who are present, regardless of whether they have been entrusted with a vote or not. In other words: whoever is in the room might as well be on the board; they are going to influence its decisions.

With the right people in the meeting room, the pastor, the chairperson, and the secretary keep the meeting on track. But how is the actual agenda of the meeting prepared? Table 13.2 lays out a model of recommended proportions to ensure that each task of governance is given its due.

TABLE 13.2 Proportionate Meeting Agendas

ITEM	PART	2 HRS	5 HRS	12 HRS
Agenda-Based Prayer & Scripture	10%	15 min	30 min	1 hr, 15 min
Board Training	25%	30 min	1 hr, 15 min	3 hrs
Accept/Revise Consent Agenda	5%	5 min	15 min	30 min
Focus of the Meeting	50%	1 hr	1 hr, 15 min	6 hrs
Status Check of Governance Tasks	5%	5 min	15 min	30 min
Concluding Thoughts & Prayer	5%	5 min	15 min	30 min

The meeting agenda, prepared by the officers and distributed in advance, keeps the game out of overtime and consists of six segments. Each meeting begins with a moment of linkage to Christ: prayer and Scripture selected by the pastor for its relevance to the agenda of the meeting. This point of departure is followed by a training component, which comprises 25% of the meeting time available. Through training, the board invests in its ability to serve with increasing excellence. Next comes the routine adoption of a consent agenda, which protects the board from wasting its time on matters that require no discussion. Then, fully half of the meeting time is given over to the focus of the meeting: a single task of governance to be addressed in depth. Following the focus, the chairperson reviews the status of non-focus governance duties, starting with the one scheduled for the next meeting. The meeting wraps up with concluding thoughts and prayer.

This proportionate approach to agenda planning helps to ensure that the board does each part of its job in a disciplined manner. Table 13.2 shows how the approximate time spent on each piece might vary from a two-hour evening meeting format, to a five-hour half-day format, to an overnight retreat including twelve hours in session. The board officers may determine that a given quarterly meeting requires a short or long format, depending on its focus.

The consent agenda is a tool that helps the board to take care of business required by external entities without busting the model of Accountable Leadership.[2] There are three kinds of proposals that the officers might decide to place on the consent agenda:

1) Actions delegated to the staff by the Guiding Principles but for which board approval is required by an outside organization, e.g. government, financial institutions, and businesses.

2) Actions that are specifically assigned to the board by the Articles of Incorporation, Bylaws, or Guiding Principles and that the officers believe the board would affirm without discussion.

3) Actions that the pastor believes to be authorized by the Guiding Principles but prefers to have the board certify in advance rather than evaluate after they are taken.

FIGURE 13.1 Consent Agenda Format

CONSENT AGENDA

Community Church of Ourtown - Quarterly Board Meeting: _____
Date

The officers of the board believe that each item below complies with the Guiding Principles and should be adopted by consent. Any item marked as questionable by a board member will be removed.

Instructions: Mark any item you believe is questionable with regard to the Guiding Principles, sign the form, and return it to the secretary or another officer prior to or upon arrival at the board meeting.

Proposal	Questionable
1._____	☐
2._____	☐
3._____	☐
4._____	☐
5._____	☐
6._____	☐
7._____	☐

I hereby vote to affirm each item above except for any I have marked as questionable.

Board Member Signature: _____ Date: _____

Figure 13.1 depicts a consent agenda format than can be used for this purpose. Note in the instructions that if a single board member marks any item as needing time for discussion, it is removed from the consent agenda prior to the recording of its adoption by the board. However, this removal does not automatically place the item on the main agenda. In some cases, the item may be dropped. In other cases, the officers may provide the board member with information outside of a meeting and follow up with an email vote. Adding the item to a meeting agenda requires advance preparation and scheduling by the chairperson.

As for preparation, the worksheet shown in Figure 13.2 is used to equip board members to deliberate on any agenda item worthy of discussion time. This advance step helps to sharpen the focus of the meeting and make the best use of the board's limited time. The worksheet is not intended for routine matters needing little or no discussion; such items belong on the consent agenda if they belong in the board meeting at all. However, each decision requiring prayerful and intelligent deliberation deserves this kind of homework ahead of time to answer questions that might otherwise waste the board's time: Is this issue an issue for the board (rather than the pastor, the staff, or the congregation), and, if so, which part of the board's job description does it fit? What is the specific ques-

FIGURE 13.2 Agenda Item Worksheet

AGENDA ITEM WORKSHEET

Community Church of Ourtown - Quarterly Board Meeting: _____
DATE

Board members may submit an item for the agenda by completing this worksheet. The chairperson will certify whether the item falls within the board's written job description and, if so, will schedule the discussion for an appropriate quarterly or special board meeting.

1. Which part of the board's job description makes this issue a board issue?

    ☐ Creating and revising our Guiding Principles

    ☐ Evaluating the pastor's progress toward fulfilling one of our Mission Principles

    ☐ Identifying a violation of one of our Boundary Principles for the pastor to rectify

    ☐ Connecting with people in our community in order to serve them ahead of ourselves

    ☐ Connecting with Christ through prayer and study of Scripture pertinent to our role

    ☐ Connecting with people in our congregation in order to help them care for one another

2. In one sentence, what is the question you want the board to address?

3. Which one of our Guiding Principles speaks most directly to this question?

4. List the alternatives you see for addressing this question and the implications of each one:

CHAIRPERSON'S INITIALS:

certified as board work _____scheduled for meeting _____distributed to board _____

---

tion/problem? (Only one per worksheet) Which Guiding Principle best speaks to this issue? What alternatives should the board consider, and what are the implications of each one? Any board member can submit an appropriate agenda item but only by doing his or her homework first.

Process for Training and Selection

It should be obvious by this point that the individuals who serve on a board using the Accountable Leadership strategy must be chosen and trained with utmost care. Board members who enter the room with a casual, mystical, or managerial expectation of tinkering with anything in the congregation that grabs their attention—or the attention of their spouses—cannot govern well. Instead, they must understand the mission, vision, values, and structure of the church; and they must understand how to provide the governance piece of that structure in alignment with the mission, vision, and values.

Table 13.3 contains a four-step process for selection of board members— referred to as trustees—that is designed to involve three of the four players in the Accountable Leadership strategy: congregation, board, and pastor. It begins with any active church member who is willing to sign a thoughtful letter of recommendation attesting to the character and commitment of the potential candidate. It ends with the senior pastor presenting to the congregation for approval a slate of individuals that the board

TABLE 13.3 Board Selection Process

1) Any member of the congregation may submit a signed letter to recommend a potential trustee of good character and commitment to the church's mission.

2) Potential trustees must successfully complete a training course taught by the senior pastor covering the mission, vision, and structure of the church.

3) Potential trustees must sign a covenant to uphold the highest standards of participation, service, supportiveness, and tithing with regard to the church.

4) The senior pastor shall present to the congregation for approval a selection of candidates that have been certified by the board as qualified to serve.

has certified. Certification is not the same thing as approval; it is the recorded recognition of the board that something or someone meets the standards contained in the Guiding Principles—in this case board member qualifications in the Accountability Principles. Between the beginning and the end of this process are two steps designed to sift the wheat from the chaff.

TABLE 13.4 Pastor's Training Course

	PRESENTATION	PREPARATION/SCREENING QUESTION
1	Mission, Vision, & Values	Do you really believe in what we're doing here?
2	Accountable Leadership	Are you willing and able to govern, not manage?
3	Mission Principles	Do you understand and support our priorities?
4	Boundary Principles	Will you defend the pastor's authority and integrity?
5	Accountability for People	Will you serve the community first, then the congregation?
6	Board Meeting Agendas	Can you work with our scheduling tools?
7	Accountability of the Pastor	Can you insist on fruitfulness and reward it well?
8	Accountability to Christ	Will you govern as a servant rather than a lord?

The pastor's course that comprises the second step of the selection process is analogous to a combination of spring training and tryouts. It is used both to orient and screen potential board members. Note in Table 13.4 the key question of screening or preparation—depending on whether the participant winds up on the board—that underlies each topic in the course. These questions reveal the character, commitment, competency, and chemistry of each potential board member.

The course screens out unsuitable would-be board members in three ways: First of all, people who do not want to take such a course are demonstrating some factor that would hinder their effectiveness as a board member, e.g. inability to make time on their calendar, lack of teachability, suspicion of the pastor's leadership agenda, or something else that

FIGURE 13.3 Sample Motion for Transition Plan

MOTION FOR TRANSITION TO AN ACCOUNTABLE LEADERSHIP STRUCTURE

Community Church of Ourtown – Special Congregational Meeting

In order to facilitate the transformation of Community Church of Ourtown as a more outward-focused and fruitful congregation, the members hereby temporarily amend the Bylaw, effective immediately, to authorize the following transition to an Accountable Leadership structure.

1. The Bylaws of Community Church shall be hereby placed in abeyance until a complete revision of the Bylaws has been recommended by the Senior Pastor and approved by the members of the congregation. Such revision shall be recommended to the congregation by the Senior Pastor no later than two years from the time that abeyance begins. If such a revision is not approved by the members within three years from the start of abeyance, the members shall vote either to discontinue the abeyance or to renew it on an annual basis as needed to complete the transition.

2. During the period of abeyance, all governmental functions described in the Bylaws shall be carried out by a Transitional Oversight Team. This Team shall be composed of the Senior Pastor and four members approved by the congregation upon recommendation of the Senior Pastor after interviews conducted with two members of the congregation whose commitment to Christ, to the new vision, and to the pastoral leadership are without question. These five Team members shall serve as the corporate officers of the church as required by law.

3. The initial four Team member recommended by the Senior Pastor are as follows: Andrew Alpha, Betty Beta, Gary Gamma, and Diane Delta. Each one has the endorsement of an interview team comprising Pastor Hiram Tuleed, Mr. Solomon A. Wiseman, and Dr. Anne N. Trepreneur. Replacement of Team members, if needed, will be done by similar process.

4. The Transitional Oversight Team shall be responsible to preserve the essential purpose, teaching, and affiliation of the church during the transition, while at the same time giving maximum freedom and support to the Senior Pastor and Staff to reinvent ministries and structures of the church as needed.

5. The role of the Senior Pastor shall be to lead the congregation to growth by guiding the Transitional Oversight Team to establish appropriate Guiding Principles for the church and by directing the Staff to manage the activities of the church within those Guiding Principles.

6. The role of the Transitional Oversight Team is to work out appropriate Guiding Principles with the Senior Pastor and to hold the Senior Pastor accountable to achieve the mission and respect the boundaries defined by those Guiding Principles.

7. The role of the Staff is to manage all the ministries and operations of the church under the direction of the Senior Pastor. Staff, whether paid or volunteer, shall be accountable to the Senior Pastor for the effectiveness of their work in terms of growth.

8. Notwithstanding the authorization of the Transitional Oversight Team to govern the church during the abeyance period, the congregation shall vote on the approval of an annual budget, the call or dismissal of the Senior Pastor, the approval of individuals recommended for service on the Transitional Oversight Team, and the purchase or sale of real property.

would hurt the work of the board. Second, after picking up information and attitudes during the course about what the pastor expects of board members, some will not want to serve. Third, when asked to sign a covenant of accountability to fulfill the commitments of a board member if selected, others will balk at the level of transparency required—especially with regard to a check of their giving records.

For the exceptional people who successfully complete the course and sign the covenant, the process will have equipped them to govern with excellence if selected. In harmony with our organizational strategy, then, the pastor leads the process of selecting board members, the board governs the process, and the congregation ministers in the process.

The Wisdom of a Transition Plan

For a congregation that is moving into Accountable Leadership from another kind of structure, the final type of scheduling equipment I will recommend is the use of a *transition plan*. Again, I caution against using a new set of bylaws as the means to introduce Accountable Leadership to a congregation that is accustomed to something else. Though logically it makes sense to start by setting up the system in the bylaws first, the real challenge is not logical; it is psychological and often pathological as well.

In terms of our sports analogy, the transition plan uses a time-out to set up new plays. This plan—enacted through a motion such as the one displayed in Figure 13.3—places the old bylaws in abeyance, or temporary suspension, for a period of two to three years prior to introducing a new set of bylaws. During the abeyance period, the congregation operates on the basis of the transition plan in order to allow for a trial run of Accountable Leadership. If Accountable Leadership proves successful, it is confirmed by the adoption of new bylaws. If the transition plan does not produce growth within three years, the congregation can either allow more time or else have the old system back in place. The essence of the Accountable Leadership strategy is incorporated into the transition plan on a temporary basis just as it will be incorporated into the bylaws on a permanent basis after a successful trial run is experienced. Without this trial run phase however, the attention of the key players is diverted away from mission and into structural concerns, thereby lessening the chance that the new strategy would bear early fruit. Resist the temptation to see your situation as an exception and to bypass the recommended transition plan.

No matter how well your organizational model is designed, if you don't schedule it, it isn't going to happen. So whip out your pocket calendar or your handheld computer and figure out what to do when. Whether you play down under or up over, if you strap on the chronological equipment in this chapter, it will keep your cuts and bruises to a minimum when you play in real time.

SUMMARY & PREVIEW

- *The calendar keeps the board playing governance, rather than management, with quarterly meetings, each focused on one of the board's four governing tasks.*

- *The meeting agenda, prepared by the officers in advance, keeps the game out of overtime and consists of four segments: focus, calendar, prayer, and training.*

- *The pastor's training course gives potential board members the chance to demonstrate character, commitment, competency, and chemistry.*

- *The transition plan uses a time-out to set up new plays. This plan suspends the old bylaws for a period of two to three years prior to adopting new bylaws.*

Our final chapter deals with the special factors of affiliation and closes out part 4 on having the right equipment. There we'll explore how the Accountable Leadership strategy helps to fix problems that are native to four kinds of congregations. We'll also discover suggestions on how to customize Winning on Purpose for the culture of each movement.

Notes

1. Reviewing the lead pastor's performance is explained by chapter 6, by "Keeping Score and Calling Penalties" in chapter 10, and by "Accountability Principles" in chapter 12. The board's review responsibility does not grow more complex with the growth of the church because the board continues to have but one employee to monitor. The lead pastor can and should delegate oversight as the staff grows; the larger the church, the fewer the staff the lead pastor needs to oversee directly.

2. The consent agenda is a tool also used by managing boards in an attempt to handle the overwhelming volume of operational detail. As used by a managing board, the tool often breaks down as various board members select items they wish to manage. The consent agenda is used for an entirely different purpose by a governing board; it discharges only those management items imposed upon the board by an outside authority or specifically requested by the senior pastor for advance certification. The chairperson is authorized by the Accountability Principles not to allow management items to occupy any substantial part of the board meeting's agenda; this discipline circumvents the kind of consent agenda break-downs that are routinely experienced by managing boards.

CHAPTER FOURTEEN

Affiliations Relate the Team to its League

*In the end, we will remember not the words
of our enemies, but the silence of our friends.*
Martin Luther King, Jr.

"ARE YOU CRYING? THERE'S NO CRYING IN BASEBALL!" objects Jimmy Dugan, played by Tom Hanks in *A League of Their Own*. One of the players in the wartime All-American Girls' Professional Baseball League had burst into tears after Dugan, the hard-drinking team manager, yelled about her little boy hanging around with the team. These all-female teams of the early 1940s were playing the same game as the men who had gone off to fight, but slogans like "dirt in the skirt" made it obvious that they were playing it in a very different league.

This chapter applies the Accountable Leadership strategy to four groups of church "leagues," three historic groups and one newcomer. Similar to the term *tribe*, popularized by Lyle Schaller, league is a reference to a denomination or a movement that functions like a denomination. As literal tribes can be grouped into nations, so church leagues can be grouped into broad traditions. Each of the Christian traditions covered in the following pages (with unavoidably broad generalizations) comes with unique challenges and opportunities for its congregations that want to win on purpose.

Winning in the Congregational Leagues

Within the tradition of congregational polity, Accountable Leadership helps autonomous local churches—e.g. Baptist, Free Church, Mennonite, Church of God (Anderson, Indiana), Congregational, and some Lutherans—to avoid inherent problems of democracy we identified earlier. The strategy also redeems a valuable heritage within congregational leagues. To best serve these movements, however, the strategy must be customized to fit the context. The left hand column in Table 14.1 shows three benefits that Accountable Leadership brings especially to churches of the congregational persuasion. The right hand column shows three ways our strategy must be customized to best serve congregational leagues. (An item on the right does not correspond to the benefit on its left.)

TABLE 14.1 Accountable Leadership With Congregational Polity

SPECIAL BENEFITS	SPECIAL CUSTOMIZATIONS
A tendency toward divisive politics is minimized.	Congregational meetings must be redeemed for mission.
The heritage of every-member-ministry is redeemed.	The autonomy of each congregation must be respected and navigated.
Control by the lowest common denominator is eliminated.	An extra measure of cultural allegiance must be addressed.

Face it: congregational church government is famous for its fights. Nothing is wrong with robust discussion or debate, but when leadership is exercised more from the floor than from the pulpit, the spirit of Christ can be quenched by a politically charged atmosphere. Accountable Leadership minimizes the tendency toward divisive politics by building a culture of trust in pastoral leadership and pointing the congregation toward ministries rather than meetings.

Speaking of ministries, a second special benefit for congregational leagues using *Winning on Purpose* is a redemption of its grassroots lay ministry. As depicted in 1 Corinthians 12, every member of the body of Christ is designed and placed in the body to serve in a unique way. The heritage of congregational polity at its best is one in which the people take ministry—not Roberts' Rules of Order—into their own hands. Accountable Leadership makes room for the congregation to have the final say on who is entrusted with leadership and whether to affirm their most far-reaching decisions. However, the emphasis is overwhelmingly on the members being ministers rather than voters.

The third benefit special to congregational churches is the elimination of control by the lowest common denominator. If a congregation is healthy and growing, it will be composed of people at all points along their spiritual journeys. Some will be long-term Christians who are walking in active obedience to God's purposes for his Church. More will be long-term Christians who are long on knowledge and short on ministry. There will be newer followers of Christ who have more knowledge to gain but are already mature in their obedience. There will also be newer followers who are still in the early stages of learning how to obey. And, despite professions to the contrary, there will be some church members who have no real personal relationship with Christ. Finally, there will be uncommitted churchgoers who are either exploring the faith or who come because they like the atmosphere. All this is normal. Nevertheless, if the vision of the ministry can only be as strong for Christ as the votes of its weakest links, it is in trouble. Accountable Leadership creates a safer place for the whole spectrum of spiritual growth without sacrificing a God-shaped and God-sized vision for the church.

The first customization on Table 14.1 is that congregational meetings must be redeemed for mission. The old-fashioned quarterly or (gulp) monthly business meeting is often spent going over committee reports about lots of intentions, several activities, and few results—that is when the meeting isn't dominated by hashing and rehashing a motion that someone made from the floor. To apply Accountable Leadership well in a context that operates like a town hall meeting, the leadership must refocus such gatherings on the mission of the church. That means fewer meetings—an annual meeting plus the occasion special meeting is sufficient—so that ministry gets more of the calendar. It also means devoting most of the annual meeting to celebrating last year's fruit (changed lives) and next year's vision (more changed lives). Voting should not be presented as either a rubber-stamp or a debate but as a hearty "Amen!" to fruitful and ethical leadership, which has been supported and monitored by the Accountable Leadership strategy throughout the year.

The second customization for congregational polity is that the autonomy of each local church must be respected and navigated. For example, in the American Baptist Churches of the West, when a congregation needs to search for a new senior pastor, the regional staff comes in with influence but not with authority. Nevertheless, the way that influence is used is critical. We give the congregation two options for our help: the traditional track of sifting through a stack of resumes from candidates who need a job, or Growth Track. In Growth Track, the congregation has to make a number of changes and commitments before we will recommend them to proven winners that we recruit from all over the country. The choice belongs to the congregation, so autonomy is respected; but in most cases, when people understand how much value we will add, the congregation chooses to grant us the authority to act in its best interests.

A third customization is to recognize and address a higher level of allegiance to this league than is often present in others. Because there is only a loose structural connection among congregational churches, the glue that holds them together tends to be loyalty rather than authority. It may manifest as a reluctance to partner with other denominations, or to use material apart from their own publishers. In terms of implementing a creative new strategy like Accountable Leadership, it is likely to manifest through questions like: "This isn't a very Baptist way of doing things, is it?" Leaders who want to transition to Accountable Leadership need to be ready with an answer.

Winning in the Presbyterian Leagues

Next we turn our attention to the spiritual descendents of John Knox, the Scottish reformer and "commissioner" of the presbyterian leagues, where it's all about the elders. Presently, there are two versions of presbyterian polity on the scene: independent and connectional. Independent presbyterian leagues would include Brethren denominations, some Reformed Baptists, many independent "Bible" churches or "community" churches, and a smattering of nonconforming affiliates within congregational denominations who have opted locally for elder-rule to one degree or another. Connectional presbyterians would naturally include the denominations called Presbyterian but would also include Nazarene, Assemblies of God, and Reformed Church in America.

TABLE 14.2 Accountable Leadership with Presbyterian Polity

SPECIAL BENEFITS	SPECIAL CUSTOMIZATIONS
For independent congregations, the elders' minimal accountability is offset.	Assumptions about "biblical eldership" must be addressed.
For connectional congregations, the heritage of pastoral oversight is redeemed.	For connectional congregations, ecclesiastical courts must be considered.
Tendency toward groupthink is minimized.	The designation and deployment of elders must be worked out.

The left column of Table 14.2 notes that correcting the minimal accountability of the elder board in independent presbyterian polity is the first special benefit that *Winning on Purpose* can bring to these churches. Without submission to the higher outside *presbytery* or *classis* that characterizes connectional Presbyterian bodies, leadership by a "plurality of elders" represents a far less accountable form of church government. Therefore, the Accountable Leadership strategy can bring a vital missing element to congregations with an independent presbyterian structure.

Next on the list of special benefits for the connectional branch, the strategy redeems the heritage of pastoral oversight that represents presbyterian polity at its best. In such denominations, the pastor of a local congregation presides over a board of elders, or *session,* and over congregational meetings. *Winning on Purpose* can be used to put fresh wind in the sails of pastoral leadership by picking up on mechanisms already in the system and retooling them with Guiding Principles to focus the accountability structures on fruitful mission.

The third way that Accountable Leadership benefits churches with presbyterian polity is through its design for individual responsibility and authority. This is a needed antidote for the groupthink that infects many elder boards. Although everyone on the board is part of a team and although the team needs to come together to speak with one voice, the team does not work without having a captain. With respect to the purposes of the board, the pastor serves as captain. With respect to the process of the board, the chairperson takes charge. But there is always an individual, not a group, that is held accountable for what happens. Thus, the board is not allowed to become a hideout for controllers who are surreptitiously calling the shots; nor does it become some mysterious entity that makes decisions in God's name but shields each of its members from having to answer for those decisions.

Now on to the special customizations that we will need to win in the presbyterian leagues. First on the right hand column of Figure 14.2 is the fact that assumptions about "biblical eldership" must frequently be addressed in congregations with presbyterian polity. This challenge may be greater for the independent variety of these leagues because they tend to be less conscious of church history, which might otherwise bring a measure of humility about the origin of their polity. One may need to sensitively explain that there are no bylaws in the New Testament; that *elder* is neither more nor less a biblical designation than *supervisor, overseer, pastor, shepherd,* or *bishop;* and that no New Testament congregation ever had a board of elders, or a board of any other kind.

A second customization is for denominations with the connectional form of presbyterian government. The subordinate relationship of the local pastor and elders to higher courts such as the classis or presbytery and further steps up to the synod and general assembly must be accommodated as prescribed in the league's book of order. However, despite the way the polity works on paper, custom and human dynamics determine how it works among people. It is common for connectional presbyterian churches to function in a largely congregational style at the local level. So the connectional customization cuts both ways: a) A congregation adopting Accountable Leadership will need to evaluate the implications for how the congregation relates to a regional court. b) A regional body adopting Accountable Leadership for itself and promoting it to its congregations will need to evaluate the most judicious use of its authority and influence.

The third customization on Table 14.2 pertains to congregations of either independent or connectional pedigree. How are the "elders" to be deployed in the Accountable Leadership strategy? Here are a few options: a) Retain the traditional title and placement of elders but define the task of the session or board purely as governance, not management. b) Create an accountability team without ecclesiastical titles to play the position of governance in the strategy, and develop the elders as a team of pastors working for the senior pastor—calling them elders whenever necessary and pastors whenever possible. c) As a new or restructured congregation, organize with entirely functional rather than ecclesiastical titles; if connectional, either fly under the radar or else give higher echelons the occasional nod when required.

Winning in the Episcopal Leagues

Leagues organized with bishops include Anglicans, Episcopalians, Salvation Army, Church of God in Christ, Orthodox, Catholic, Foursquare, mainline Methodists and Lutherans, and to some degree newer "apostolic" movements like Calvary Chapels and Vineyard. We turn now to the application of *Winning on Purpose* to the episcopal leagues.

TABLE 14.3 Accountable Leadership with Episcopal Polity

SPECIAL BENEFITS	SPECIAL CUSTOMIZATIONS
Intellection is put into action—so that the ivory tower is also a spiritual lighthouse.	Creative incentives must be designed for a context of guaranteed appointment.
Heritage of spiritual authority and submission is redeemed.	Frequent reassignments require tactics to leverage or extend short pastorates.
The mission of the church flows from the liturgy of the church.	The book of church discipline must be accommodated or benignly neglected.

The first special benefit in Table 14.3 is transforming a value on intellection into missional action. A high-church culture, at least in developed nations, tends toward a more intellectual approach to faith. Accountable Leadership offers these leagues a tool for turning brainpower toward fruitful service.

Despite the fact that the local parish may act nearly autonomously much of the time, the episcopal leagues do preserve a rich heritage of spiritual authority and submission—biblical principles somewhat foreign to modern and postmodern values. The strategy in this book can help redeem this legacy, not to glorify the clergy but to glorify the Father by bearing much fruit (John 15:8). This redemption is a second special benefit for episcopal denominations. If someone has been entrusted with a place of authority, that person can use it either to stimulate mission or stifle it. Where much has been given, much will be required.

Many, but not all, episcopal leagues practice the ancient four-part pattern of Christian liturgy, which has been formalized since the fourth century. To the sense of beauty and mystery that the liturgy entails (Entrance, Proclamation and Response, Thanksgiving and Communion, Sending Forth), Accountable Leadership adds a practical strategy for mission to ensure that Sending Forth amounts to more than good intentions. Isaiah 6 records the vision of the Lord high and lifted up and ends with the obedience of "Here am I, send me." Worship without obedience is repugnant to God, according to Isaiah 1:13, but a congregation fueled by a sense of Jesus's presence and obedient to Jesus's commission is a mighty force for the Kingdom of God. As John Wesley would agree, what good is apostolic succession without apostolic (or missionary) action?

The nature of the call to pastoral ministry in a number of episcopal denominations entails a promise, or at least an expectation, of guaranteed placement, once fully accepted as permanent clergy. This feature of the landscape poses a challenge for accountability if you will always have one appointment or another no matter how poorly you execute its duties. For this reason, creative incentives must be designed to reward fruitfulness and to penalize incompetence. The shape of these reinforcements is determined by the authority or influence of those who are bringing Accountable Leadership to bear. A local vestry might enhance compensation or sabbatical leave. A bishop or district superintendent might create an advanced leadership track. If you are the national primate, you might have sufficient authority to redesign the entire placement system.

Speaking of placement, we come to the second customization needed for the episcopal leagues: tactics to either extend or else leverage shorter pastorates. The good thing about having bishops is their ability to move pastors around. The bad thing about having bishops is their ability to move pastors around. Typically, this means that weak performers play musical chairs. In the case where a congregation gets a strong performer to lead the team, just as the points start going up on the scoreboard, its captain may be reassigned, either randomly or—perhaps worse—as a reward for doing well. To counter the ill effects of this practice, one must either derail it or redeem it. Perhaps a parish that wants to keep its effective pastor can negotiate extra support of the diocese in exchange. If an extension is not possible, perhaps a vestry can learn best practices from other enterprises that must thrive under replaceable leadership, e.g. battlefield commanders in military units.

Finally, similar to our discussion of connectional presbyterian leagues, Accountable Leadership functioning in a hierarchy must either accommodate the official book of church order or else treat it with benign neglect. This customization of the strategy requires that mandated structures, which realistically cannot be replaced, be redeemed or redefined if possible. If not, they should be marginalized in favor of unofficial shadow structures that are created to provide what the official structures should provide but cannot.

Winning in the Emerging Leagues

There are movements afoot in recent years that deserve separate treatment, though the congregations within them may overlap with historical patterns. We will call them the emerging leagues. At different times these ministries have been labeled Gen-X, Postmodern, Emerging, Emergent, and Missional. They represent part culture-shift, part pendulum-swing, part spiritual-quest, and part next-big-thing. Because these leagues are morphing rapidly toward an unknown future, it is easier to define what they are not: not modern, not linear, not megachurch, not seeker-sensitive, not Boomer, not traditional, not contemporary, not corporate, not slick, and most definitely not "a vendor of religious goods and services."[1] Dan Kimball suggests post-seeker-sensitive and "vintage Christianity for emerging generations."[2] Values include spirituality, community, cultural relevance, the arts, authenticity, and mission. These leagues have no one organizational model but rather "flexible and resilient structures that allow us to encounter, influence, evangelize, equip, and empower people effectively as authentic disciples sent into the rapids of societal change as emissaries of God."[3] So I will speak not of their polity but of their "unpolity."

TABLE 14.4 Accountable Leadership with Emergent "Unpolity"

SPECIAL BENEFITS	SPECIAL CUSTOMIZATIONS
A helpful measure of order is added to the creative chaos, enhancing its value.	Metaphors associated with business and modernity must be used with discretion.
Missional presence that might be diffused becomes accountable for fruitfulness.	Bones of organizational structure must be covered with lots of spiritual muscle.
Common ground is created with moderns to get beyond anger and into partnership.	Extra flexibility must be designed in to accommodate a fast-changing movement.

The first special benefit that Accountable Leadership offers to the emerging leagues is a helpful measure of order added to the creative chaos. The strategy is flexible enough to apply in a variety of contexts and malleable enough to adapt with constant change. Creative chaos can be a strength as long as there is more creativity than chaos.

A second benefit special to emerging leagues is that their missional presence in the community, which might otherwise be diffused and ineffectual, is redeemed through accountability for bearing much fruit. Missional churches that care about transforming lives and communities are given a useful tool to help them stay on track. Missional churches of the random-acts-of-kindness variety are offered a mirror to challenge them to make a measurable difference in the world.

Now to a more sensitive matter: Insiders of the emerging leagues are aware that a certain amount of pain and anger fuels a part (and only a part) of the passion to reject all things Boomer and Modern. Leaders hurt or disenfranchised by established churches translate a portion of their pathology into missiology. There is more than just a philosophical or theological difference at work; broken relationships figure into the equation. Therefore, a third benefit that the Accountable Leadership strategy can bring to emerging leagues is creating common missional ground between "moderns" and "postmoderns" to get past the anger and into fruitful partnerships for the gospel—without compromising values.

Turning to the customizations of the strategy that are needed for the emerging leagues, let us begin with the matter of presentation: Metaphors associated with modernity, business, or megachurches must be used with discretion. I am not suggesting that the distinctives of the emerging leagues are merely a matter of style and language; they are not. I am suggesting that leaders of these ministries may not recognize the radical commitment to biblical mission represented by Accountable Leadership if they only see it wrapped in the metaphors of modernity. *Winning on Purpose* uses sports as its dominant metaphor because athletic language is generally clear and acceptable to people of all the leagues, generations, and movements this book was written to assist.

A second customization for the emerging leagues is to cover the structural bones of the strategy with a great deal of spiritual muscle. Missional church leaders do not get excited about some nifty new organizational model; they get excited about cooperating with the purposes of God in the world. Other leagues would do well to learn this priority from them. So for Accountable Leadership to be most helpful to the emerging or missional church, it must be lean (e.g. shorter Guiding Principles, in more radical ministries not longer than the comprehensive mission, boundary, and accountability statements perhaps), it must be discreet (i.e. carefully applied in the background not the foreground), and above all it must be submitted to the Spirit and Word of God.

Finally, the application of Accountable Leadership to an emerging congregation must be designed with extra flexibility, using functional rather than traditional structures. One fast-growing emerging church in Tallahassee that I have worked with calls its staff the ARA Team to highlight full Authority, full Responsibility, and full Accountability. If they need to morph the structure sometime, the "ARA Team" is going to be less of a sacred cow to change than a "Board of Deacons" would be.

Affiliation equips the congregational team with a larger league, whether formally or informally. There are hundreds of ecclesiastical leagues, each with a different culture, and we cannot even begin to address here the variables of place, ethnicity, socioeconomic factors, and generation. Unlike Jimmy Dugan's baseball, in ministry we cannot say that there's no crying. But we'll shed fewer tears for the wrong reasons if we'll hold leaders accountable for mission within a league of their own.

SUMMARY

- *Accountable Leadership can help the congregational leagues avoid problems of democracy and redeem their grassroots ministry.*

- *Accountable Leadership can help the presbyterian leagues avoid problems of oligarchy and redeem their pastoral oversight.*

- *Accountable Leadership can help the episcopal leagues avoid problems of bureaucracy and redeem their spiritual authority.*

- *Accountable Leadership can help the emerging leagues avoid problems of anarchy and redeem their missional fruitfulness.*

Notes

1. Darrell Guder, ed., *The Missional Church: A Vision for the Sending of the Church in North America* (Grand Rapids: Eerdmans, 1998), 79–82.

2. Dan Kimball, *The Emerging Church: Vintage Christianity for New Generations* (Grand Rapids: Zondervan, 2003), 31–38.

3. Milfred Minatrea, *Shaped by God's Heart: The Passion and Practices of Missional Churches* (San Francisco: Jossey-Bass, 2004), 144.

CONCLUSION

AMERICANS CALL THEM "ARMCHAIR QUARTERBACKS." Pudgy, middle-aged men with a beer in one hand and a TV remote in the other can call a better play than their counterparts on the field—after the instant replay. Congregations are filled with spiritual armchair quarterbacks. Pastors whose flocks are not growing take potshots at those who are more successful. Decline becomes evidence of faithfulness. Sermons about the remnant outnumber sermons about reaching Jerusalem, Judea, Samaria, and the uttermost parts. Boards and congregations support incompetent pastors who do as they are told, and run off visionary pastors who try to raise the bar. Leading a North American congregation to grow is hard work that requires a pastor to fight the good fight against the odds since most congregations on that continent are not growing. Boards and members that pick a winning quarterback and run interference, rather than create it, are not guaranteed a win every time. However, through dedication to the Great Commission, trust in a proven pastoral leader, and accountability for results, they can reverse the odds in their favor.

Strategy Recap

The first question we face is whether or not we really want to win as a congregation or a pastor. It is so much easier to pooh-pooh those who strive for results as worldly, compromising, ambitious, corporate, modern, or whatever adjective is currently out of favor in the Christian subculture. As Paul wrote to the Corinthians, God is the only one who gives the increase. And there is no question about *God's* faithfulness. But what about *ours?* Are we serious about laying a foundation and taking care how we build on it? Or are we more comfortable with our false humility and true irresponsibility about the active part God calls us to play in the only game that matters forever?

If we are indeed serious about leading congregations to win on *purpose* at *their purpose, we must know what that purpose is.* For disciples of Jesus, the first and final word on the matter is to reproduce more disciples. Along with the apostles, we are called to "fish for people" and to "make disciples" (learners) of all nations, whether they come to us as on the day of Pentecost, or whether we go to them as on the journeys of Paul. With the ease of immigration, travel, and global communications today, there are ample opportunities in both directions.

To empower leaders for safe and effective performance, we must establish a few simple boundaries. When the rules of the game are clear and concise, the best players can rise to the challenge with all of their passion and creativity. Authorization for any tactic within the rules promotes far more fruitfulness than the typical approval of recommendations used in slow-growth or no-growth congregations.

Accountability is how we keep score. To determine whether or not the object of the game is being achieved and whether or not the boundaries are being respected, someone has to check from time to time and to give the leader appropriate feedback based on what has actually been happening. This concept is not foreign to God. Jesus himself spoke on one occasion of uprooting the barren fig tree and on another of doubling the talents entrusted to productive stewards. But the concept is foreign to many congregations that claim to represent God.

The strategy this book offers to help congregations set up their pastors for success is Accountable Leadership. It can be summarized in four points: The role of the board is to govern. The role of the pastor is to lead. The role of the staff is to manage. The role of the congregation is to minister.

Finally, to implement Accountable Leadership well, congregations and pastors must have the right equipment and must gain skill in using it. Organizational documents, particularly the Guiding Principles, that the board creates and recreates play an essential role. To make the most of time, our most precious commodity, we must also equip ourselves with scheduling tools that work out the strategy in hours and years. The league in which we play equips us with a certain context to consider. Accountable Leadership can help congregations of any polity or "unpolity," if the strategy is customized, to bring out the best and counter the worst traits of each context.

Beyond the Local Congregation

This volume has been written specifically for the local congregation. The Church is the entity established by Christ and assured of ultimate victory against the gates of hell. However, it should be obvious to thoughtful readers that the principles in *Winning on Purpose* are readily adaptable to other types of ministry organizations.

Denominational judicatories can win on purpose. Would you like to turn the Peter Principle on its head and live down the reputation of denominational executives as paper-pushers? (Q: "How many people work at our national headquarters?" A: "About a third of them.") Try a good dose of accountability. But you better have the right transition plan and backup support before you start. Investing in what works and abandoning what doesn't is not the way to make a lot of friends in a stagnant organization. It's strong medicine, so hire an organizational doctor who has seen your dysfunction before and knows what course of therapy to prescribe. Just as a winning congregation requires a winning senior pastor, a winning judicatory requires a winning executive minister. Accountable Leadership helps identify winners and optimize their results; it doesn't create winners.

Mission agencies can win on purpose. Theoretically, mission agencies should be much further ahead than congregations in terms of outward focus and accountability for results. And sometimes they are. But often, missionaries are supported based on needs rather than fruit. This is not best for either the missionaries or the mission because we tend to get more of whatever we subsidize. The cause of Christ is better served if we search for newsletters with more about the latest new disciples and less about the latest new hassles of the missionaries. Let's continue to pray for both, but let's write bigger checks to the former. Effective missionaries should get *more* support and the others should be weeded out. Anyone out there serious about winning the world?

Parachurch organizations can win on purpose. Especially in the era following World War II, spiritual entrepreneurs like Bill Bright of Campus Crusade for Christ and Dawson Trotman of The Navigators sprang forward to seize opportunities that congregations were too slow to recognize. They formed ministries alongside (*para*) the church to reach those whom the church was not reaching. Today, some of the most effective pastors of high impact churches cut their teeth either as parachurch staff or in similar evangelistic youth ministries. Because the parachurch arena is all about fruit, it is a natural fit with the Accountable Leadership strategy.

Training and Consulting

Readers, writers, and publishers each have limits for how much material makes sense for one book. And so *Winning on Purpose* is not an exhaustive treatment of the Accountable Leadership strategy. It is, however, a reasoned, passionate argument, a clear presentation of the components of the strategy, and a suggestion of some starting points for implementation.Each congregation, denomination, and nonprofit organization with which I have worked has brought a unique set of obstacles and opportunities for missional success. There is no way to do justice within the scope of this book to the variables of each denomination and movement in the Church of Jesus Christ. That will be up to individual readers, future publications, and professional consultation to address.

To do further study and application, please refer to the annotated bibliography. You won't find the Accountable Leadership strategy as a whole in any of the books recommended in the bibliography, but you will find pieces of it or influences on it among them. The index will help you navigate *Winning on Purpose* as a handbook for Accountable Leadership.

I plan to produce further publications in a variety of media to help implement Accountable Leadership. The best way to check the progress of these publications is to visit the website: www.accountableleadership.org. You will also find up-to-date news and contact information.

Like anyone else in ministry, my time is limited. However, I do enjoy training and consulting with leaders who are serious about advancing the Great Commission. If your congregation, denomination, or nonprofit organization would like support, please feel free to contact me through the website or through Abingdon Press. If I can't arrange to help you personally, I'll put you together with someone who can.

Jesus Wins

An old story tells of a pastor who noticed from his office window that the aging church custodian ate his lunch each day under a tree with an open Bible on his lap. One day he wandered outside to say hello and was amazed to see the custodian's Bible opened up to the book of Revelation. "Do you actually understand what that book means?" the pastor asked. "Sure do," replied the custodian, swallowing the last bite of his sandwich, "It means Jesus is gonna win."

And so it does. While there is an urgency about making disciples while we are still deployed on earth, it does not spring from any doubt concerning who will ultimately prevail. Christ will build his church, and the gates of hell will not prevail against it. So the urgency arises from our own limitations. Worship, community, instruction, and prayer will be ours forever—better after this life than ever. But when our time on earth is over, we will never again see people pass from death to life. We will never again make a disciple. Jesus wins—that much we know. What remains to be seen is who will be there to celebrate with him at the awards banquet.

Annotated Bibliography

Anderson, Leith. *Leadership That Works: Hope and Direction for Church and Parachurch Leaders in Today's Complex World*. Minneapolis: Bethany House, 2002.
Lyle Schaller has called Leith Anderson the "wisest pastor in America." Anderson's book paints a realistic picture of the challenges of pastoral leadership in the typical congregation, not just the megachurch—though it applies there as readily. It offers practical and transferable principles about what to do.

Andringa, Robert C., and Ted W. Engstrom. *Nonprofit Board Answer Book: Practical Guidelines for Board Members and Chief Executives*. Washington DC: National Center for Nonprofit Boards, 1997.
This is a handbook of nuts and bolts for good board practice. It is not linked to a particular strategy, so ignore the nuts and bolts pertaining only to a managing board.

Bandy, Thomas G. *Christian Chaos: Revolutionizing the Congregation*. Nashville: Abingdon, 1999.
Bandy and I share a strong aversion to the dysfunctional structures that plague churches. Both of us have also been influenced by John Carver's model though neither of us believes it fits the nature of the church. However, Bandy's alternative to Carver is based on teams rather than leaders, while mine is based on leaders held accountable for their teams.

Bennis, Warren and Burt Nanus. *Leaders: The Strategies for Taking Charge*. New York: Harper & Row, 1985.
Bennis and Nanus is a classic on leadership vs. management. It remains a valuable handbook on how to lead in any context, including the church.

Block, Stephen R. *Perfect Nonprofit Boards: Myths, Paradoxes, and Paradigms*. Needham Heights, MA: Simon & Schuster, 1998.
Block propounds the "executive director-concerted" model. Like Accountable Leadership, and unlike the Carver model, Block recognizes that the organization needs its executive to lead the board as well as the staff.

Borden, Paul D. *Hit the Bullseye: How Denominations Can Aim the Congregation toward the Mission Field*. Nashville: Abingdon, 2003.
Borden is my mentor and the greatest single influence on my development of the Accountable Leadership strategy. *Hit the Bullseye* is not a theory but the true story of a judicatory that achieved an unprecedented turnaround through the courageous application of accountability to pastoral leadership.

Bossidy, Larry and Ram Charan. *Execution: The Discipline of Getting Things Done*. New York: Crown Business, 2002.
Excellence in management is just as important as excellence in leadership. Bossidy and Charan, though writing for business, can help pastors inebriated at the vision bar to wake up and smell the coffee of implementation.

Buckingham, Marcus and Donald O. Clifton. *Now Discover Your Strengths.* New York: Free Press, 2001.
The StrengthsFinder profile, based on Gallup research, shows the value of focusing rather than balancing one's personal energy. The book includes an online profile.

Callahan, Kennon L. *Twelve Keys to an Effective Church: Strategic Planning for Mission.* San Francisco: HarperSanFrancisco, 1983.
Callahan's keys can unlock the doors of established churches to outward focused mission. His "relational" keys are: 1) missional objectives, 2) pastoral and lay visitation, 3) corporate, dynamic worship, 4) significant relational groups, 5) strong leadership resources, and 6) streamlined structure. His "functional" keys are: 1) several competent programs and activities, 2) open accessibility, 3) high visibility, 4) adequate parking, land, and landscaping, 5) adequate space and facilities, 6) solid financial resources. Callahan's sequel, *Effective Church Leadership,* is even better.

Carver, John. *Boards that Make a Difference: A New Design for Leadership in Nonprofit and Public Organizations.* 2nd ed. San Francisco: Jossey-Bass, 1997.
Carver's Policy Governance model is provocative, brilliant, insightful, and in my opinion fatally flawed—at least for church application. Over the years my own work evolved from application to adaptation to finally creating an alternative. The most profound difference between Accountable Leadership and Policy Governance is the positioning of the senior pastor. Carver would exclude the pastor from the board and therefore from decisions on mission and boundaries. That exclusion is antithetical to a senior pastor as the primary spiritual leader of a congregation in any biblical sense.

Collins, Jim. *Good to Great: Why Some Companies Make the Leap...and Others Don't.* New York: Harper Business, 2001.
Collins's *Built to Last* was good, but this sequel is great! His research showed companies excel not by diversifying but by concentrating their energies.

Cordeiro, Wayne. *Doing Church as a Team.* Ventura, CA: Regal, 2001.
Cordeiro's book is helpful, but if you can, hang out at New Hope Christian Fellowship in person. For all of the good stuff on teamwork, Cordeiro is a strong leader who attracts strong leaders around him. He's a good writer but even better practitioner. If you can't get to Honolulu, surf to www.enewhope.org.

Easum, Bill, and Dave Travis. *Beyond the Box: Innovative Churches that Work.* Loveland, CO: Group Publishing, 2003.
Thinking outside the box became the box, so Easum and Travis talk beyond the box. Next book: *We Don't Need No Stinkin' Box!* Metaphor inflation aside, if you like to learn from effective congregations, this book can save you some airline tickets. But watch out for a straw-man argument in chapter 1, "Beyond One-Person Leadership: Shifting to Teams." The examples throughout the book, including those in chapter 1, undercut the authors' "team leadership" bias; no thriving congregation they cite lacks a strong senior pastor.

Getz, Gene A. *Elders and Leaders: God's Plan for Leading the Church.* Chicago: Moody, 2003.
Previous bouts of Elderitis Pluralis (inflammation of the elders) from the 1st

ed. of Getz' *Sharpening the Focus of the Church* left their mark. However, he recovered nicely from this malady and has written an exegetical treatise on the need for a primary pastoral leader. This book marks a long philosophical journey from his first edition.

Guder, Darrell L., ed. *Missional Church: A Vision for the Sending of the Church in North America.* Grand Rapids: Eerdmans, 1998.
Guder provides a theological foundation for Emerging Church and Missional Church movements. It is not a how-to book but a why-to book. On p. 239, a few strategies appear but only as an end in themselves without accountability for bearing fruit: "In this diversity of structures, the gospel will be witnessed to, the rule of Christ will be announced and practiced, and the ecclesial practices will take place."

Houle, Cyril O. *Governing Boards: Their Nature and Nurture.* San Francisco: Jossey-Bass, 1997.
If you want a base line from which to evaluate innovative models of governance, Houle provides a well-written, up-to-date description of traditional nonprofit boards.

Jackson, John. *PastorPreneur: Pastors and Entrepreneurs Answer the Call.* Friendswood, TX: Baxter Press, 2003.
Carson Valley Christian Center was planted in 1998, grew to 1,000 in two years and to 2,000 in five. Jackson, the founding pastor, offers five strategies for succeeding at mission. He personifies Accountable Leadership and knows how to win on purpose.

Kimball, Dan. *The Emerging Church: Vintage Christianity for New Generations.* Grand Rapids: Zondervan, 2003.
Kimball provides a clear and convincing case for a fresh expression of biblical Christianity, contextualized for new generations. Even better, he makes the case without a hint of the reactionary anger or revisionist theology that has tended to mark some movers and shakers in the Emergent Church and Missional Church movements.

Malphurs, Aubrey. *Planting Growing Churches for the 21st Century: A Comprehensive Guide for New Churches and Those Desiring Renewal.* 3rd ed. Grand Rapids: Baker, 2004.
Malphurs is a prolific writer who compiles the best principles and practices from healthy, growing, and reproducing congregations.

Maxwell, John. *The 21 Irrefutable Laws of Leadership: Follow Them and People Will Follow You.* Nashville: Thomas Nelson, 1998.
Maxwell is a larger than life personality who is beyond prolific as a writer. (I suspect a wireless connection of brain synapses to printing presses.) Style and marketing aside, his principles of leadership are insightful from both a biblical and practical perspective.

McIntosh, Gary L. *Biblical Church Growth: How You Can Work with God to Build a Faithful Church.* Grand Rapids: Baker, 2003.
In his leadership books, McIntosh knows how to address either the how-tos or the why-tos of effective congregational ministry. This volume blends the two. By taking church growth back down to its missional roots with McGavran in

India, McIntosh recaptures its original intent as a synonym for effective evangelism.

Minatrea, Milfred. *Shaped by God's Heart: The Passion and Practices of Missional Churches.* San Francisco: Jossey-Bass, 2004.
Minatrea has done the Missional Church movement and the body of Christ a great service with this work. The book is clear and compelling about what matters most. Like Kimball, he represents the best of emergent thought without a redefining of Christianity or a condescending tone toward "moderns."

Osborne, Larry W. *The Unity Factor: Developing a Healthy Church Leadership Team.* Vista, CA: Owl Concepts, 1989.
North Coast Church near San Diego pioneered the video venue strategy for multiple congregations that is being replicated all over the country. The Unity Factor contains useful tips for a healthy relationship of senior pastor with board and staff people.

Pascale, Richard T., et al. *Surfing the Edge of Chaos: The Laws of Nature and the New Laws of Business.* New York: Three Rivers Press, 2000.
This book applies complex adaptive systems in biology to the life of corporations. It counters both high-control and no-control alternatives to wise leadership in a fluid environment.

Peter, Laurence J. and Raymond Hull, *The Peter Principle.* New York: William Morrow, 1969.
An oldie but goodie, this classic cautions against the tendency of hierarchies to promote people to their level of incompetence.

Schaller, Lyle E. *The Very Large Church: New Rules for Leaders.* Nashville: Abingdon, 2000.
This book—one of Schaller's best—addresses the challenges of congregations between 750 and 1800 in attendance. It is full of insight for any leader.

Southerland, Dan. *Transitioning: Leading Your Church through Change.* Grand Rapids: Zondervan, 1999.
Southerland transitioned a traditional Southern Baptist congregation in Ft. Lauderdale to a cutting-edge megachurch—without alienating his seniors. Impressive leadership!

Warren, Rick. *The Purpose-Driven Church.* Grand Rapids: Zondervan, 1995.
Warren is probably the single most influential pastor in the world today and rightfully so. The Purpose-Driven Church is the definitive statement of Warren's ministry philosophy.

Welch, Jack, with Suzy Welch. *Winning.* New York: HarperBusiness, 2005.
Welch is the retired CEO of General Electric. The book is not a memoir but a leadership text, e.g. What Leaders Do: 1) Upgrade the team, 2) Live and breathe the vision, 3) Exude positive energy, 4) Establish trust, 5) Make courageous decisions, 6) Answer questions with action, 7) Inspire risk taking and learning, and 8) Celebrate.

Index

Authors and Titles

Movements and Ministries

Names and Places

Scripture References

About the Author

John Edmund Kaiser

In 2006, shortly after completing this book, Dr. John Kaiser became president of the Fellowship of Evangelical Baptist Churches in Canada (fellowship.ca), one of the country's larger evangelical denominations. Prior to that appointment he developed and directed GHC Network (ghcnetwork.org), a movement for growing healthy congregations, under the auspices of the American Baptist Churches of the West (growinghealthychurches.com), based in Northern California. In the 1980s and 90s, he successfully bounded and led both a midsize church and a large church in Florida with the Evangelical Free Church of America

John consults, trains, and coaches leaders of churches, nonprofit organizations, and denominations across North America, New Zealand, and Australia. He lives near Toronto awith Lee, his wife of 27 years. They have two adult children, Ben and Ruth. John holds a B.A. from Bryan College, an M.A. and M.Div. from Trinity Evangelical Divinity School, and a D.Min. from Denver Seminary

For resources and information related to John's consulting, training, and writing, check out www.accountableleadership.org